Origami
for
Playtime

SATOSHI TAKAGI

JAPAN PUBLICATIONS TRADING COMPANY

Origami de Asobo in Japanese published by Nihon Bungei-sha Co., Ltd. 1-7 Kanda Jinbo-cho, Chiyoda-ku, Tokyo 101-8407, Japan.

English translation: Kazuhiko Nagai

© 2003 English tex., Japan Publications Trading Co., Ltd.
English language edition by Japan Publications Trading Co., Ltd., 1-2-1 Sarugaku-cho, Chiyoda-ku, Tokyo 101-0064, Japan.

First edition: First printing : October 2003

Distributors:
United States: Kodansha America, Inc. through Oxford University Press, 198 Madison Avenue, New York, NY 10016, U.S.A.
Canada: Fitzhenry and Whiteside Ltd., 195 Allstate Parkway, Markham, Ontario, L3R 4T8.
United Kingdom and Europe: Premier Book Marketing Ltd., Clarendon House, 52 Cornmarket Street, Oxford OX1 3HJ, England.
Australia and New Zealand: Bookwise International Pty Ltd. 174 Cormack Road, Wingfield, South Australia 5013, Australia.
Asia and Japan: Japan Publications Trading Co., Ltd., 1-2-1 Sarugaku-cho, Chiyoda-ku, Tokyo 101-0064, Japan.

ISBN: 4-88996-131-3
Printed in Japan

Preface

Origami is a traditional art of folding square paper into various figures. It is a wonder that a variety of products are created from only a sheet of paper. The paper changes forms as it is folded, and the process is very exciting. It is a great joy when the model is completed. Introduced in this book are basic, simple and familiar 80 models. Each method is illustrated step by step. Follow the instructions carefully and you can easily master paper folding. Origami stimulates and enriches imagination and it also helps develop creativity.

Contents

Part 1 — Basic Origami

Part 2 — Living Things

Part 3
Furniture and Small Articles

Part 4
Cars, Ships, Airplanes

SYMBOLS AND BASIC FOLDS

VALLEY FOLD

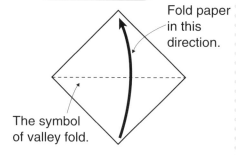

Fold paper in this direction.

The symbol of valley fold.

MOUNTAIN FOLD

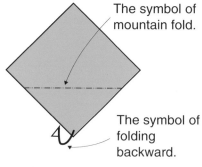

The symbol of mountain fold.

The symbol of folding backward.

1

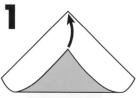

Bring the two corners together.

1

Fold the bottom edge backward.

2

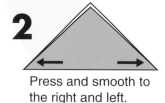

Press and smooth to the right and left.

2

Press and smooth with fingers.

PLEAT

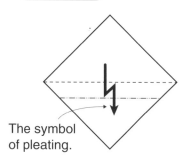

The symbol of pleating.

1

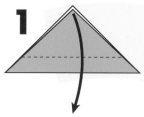

First fold by mountain fold and then fold back by valley fold.

2

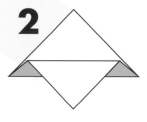

Finished.

6

INSIDE REVERSE FOLD

The symbol of inside reverse fold.

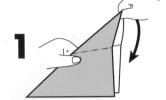

1 Hold the base with the left hand and the top corner with the right hand.

2 Fold down the corner along the creases.

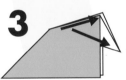

3 Press and smooth with fingers.

OUTSIDE REVERSE FOLD

The symbol of outside reverse fold.

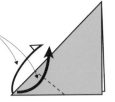

Make creases beforehand.

1 Unfold the paper and lift the corner.

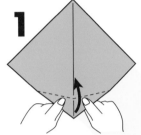

2 Shape into a correct form.

3 Press and smooth with fingers.

CREASE

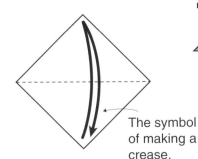

The symbol of making a crease.

1 Unfold after making a crease.

2 Symbol of the crease.

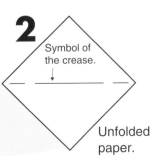

Unfolded paper.

BLOW UP

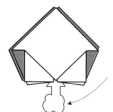

The symbol of blowing up.

1

Inflate by blowing up or using hands.

2

Shape the whole so that the lines stand out.

CUT

1

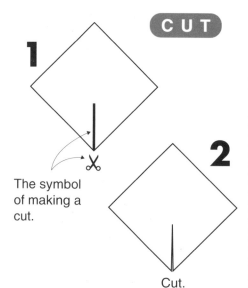

The symbol of making a cut.

2

Cut.

ROLL

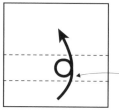

The symbol of rolling paper.

1

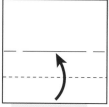

Make a crease and unfold.

2

Fold the bottom edge to the crease.

3

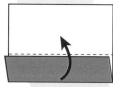

Fold again on the crease.

The symbol of enlarging.

4

It should look like this.

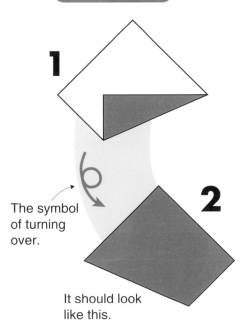

1

The symbol of turning over.

2

It should look like this.

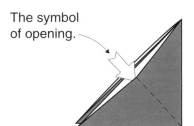

The symbol of opening.

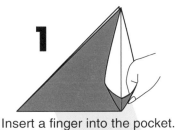

1

Insert a finger into the pocket.

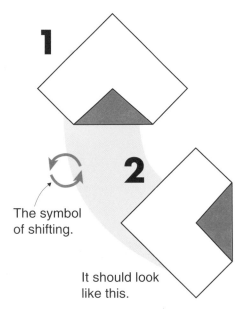

1

2

The symbol of shifting.

It should look like this.

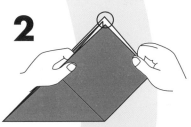

2

Let the corners meet at a ○.

3

Press and smooth in the directions of arrows.

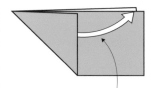

The symbol of pushing in.

The symbol of inserting.

The symbol of pulling out.

1

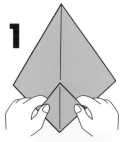

Make mountain folds and pinch the creases.

1

Open the pocket and bring the edge to the opening.

1

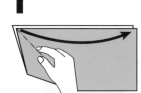

Open the upper layer.

2

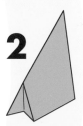

Push in by changing the center mountain fold into valley fold.

2

Insert firmly.

2

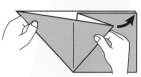

Bring the corner to the corner indicated by the arrow.

3

Press and smooth in the directions of arrows.

3

Press and smooth neatly with fingers.

3

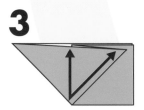

Press and smooth neatly with fingers.

Part 1
Basic Origami

You can play
alone or with your friends.

Pinwheel, Trick sailboat

Paper **Any color**

1

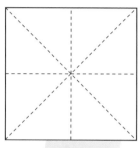

Make creases.

2

Fold in half.

Turn over.

3

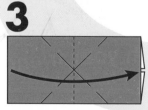

Fold in half.

Shift.

4

Make a crease.

5

Make creases.

6

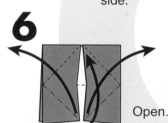

Open.

7

Repeat on the other side.

12

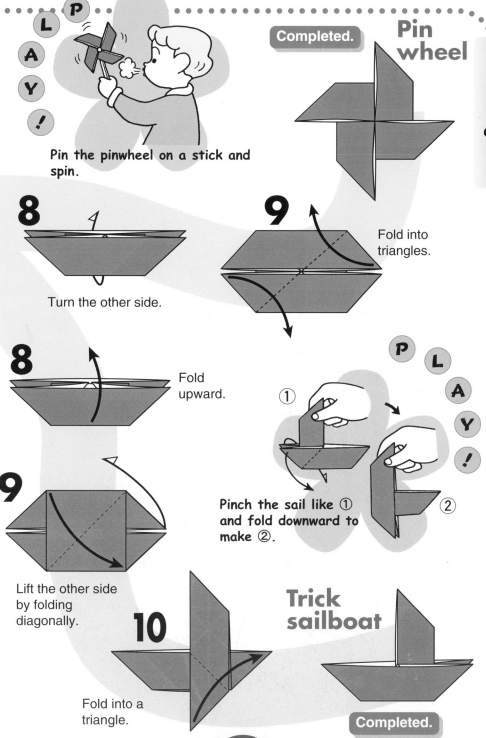

Pin wheel

Completed.

Pin the pinwheel on a stick and spin.

8

Turn the other side.

9

Fold into triangles.

8

Fold upward.

9

Lift the other side by folding diagonally.

① ②

Pinch the sail like ① and fold downward to make ②.

Trick sailboat

10

Fold into a triangle.

Completed.

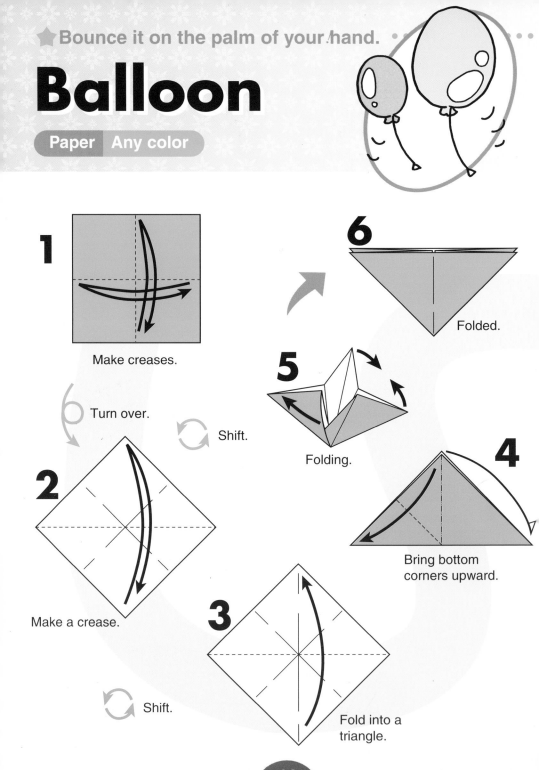

★ **Bounce it on the palm of your hand.**

Balloon

Paper | **Any color**

1 Make creases.

Turn over.

Shift.

2 Make a crease.

Shift.

3 Fold into a triangle.

4 Bring bottom corners upward.

5 Folding.

6 Folded.

14

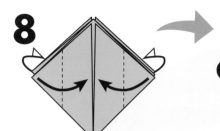

8

Bring side corners to center. Repeat on the other side.

9

Fold corners downward.

Turn over.

10

Tuck corners into the pockets.

Shift.

7

Bring bottom corners to the top point. Repeat on the other side.

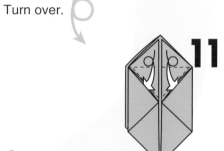

11

Repeat on the other side.

12

Blow in.

Completed.

P L A Y !

Make lovely balloons with colorful paper.

Paper gun

Paper **Newspaper**

2

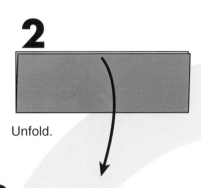

Unfold.

1

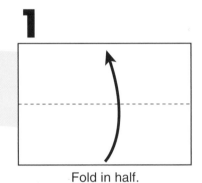

Fold in half.

3

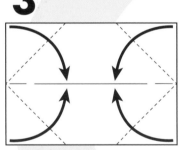

Fold corners on creases.

5

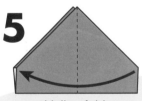

Valley fold.

Shift.

4

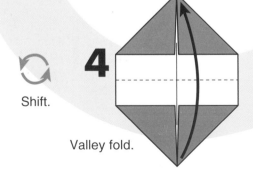

Valley fold.

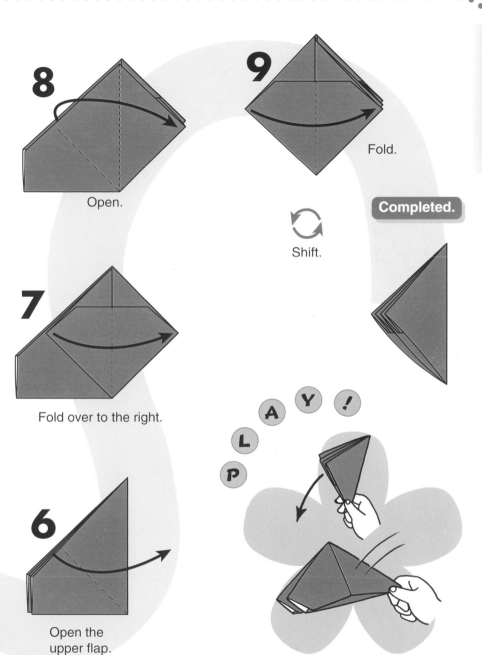

8

Open.

9

Fold.

Shift.

Completed.

7

Fold over to the right.

P L A Y !

6

Open the upper flap.

Hold the corner and bring it down with force. It will open and produce a big sound.

⭐ It works like a hand puppet.

Fox

Paper | Yellow

1

Make a crease.

2

Fold in half.

3

Unfold.

Turn over.

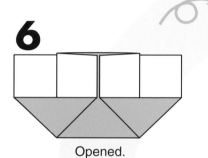

6

Opened.

5

Open.

4

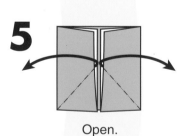

Bring both sides to center.

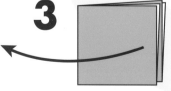

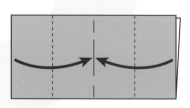

18

7

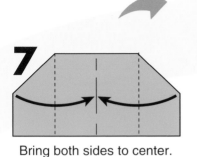

Bring both sides to center.

8

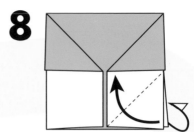

Fold into a triangle. Repeat on the other side.

9

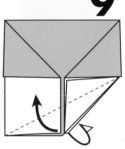

Fold diagonally. Repeat on the other side.

Shift.

10

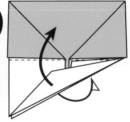

Fold the layer upward. Repeat on the other side.

11

Dent the middle with a finger.

Completed.

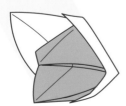

Bark and yelp !

Insert your fingers and open and close the mouth.

19

Frisbee

Paper **Any color**

Cut the paper in half.

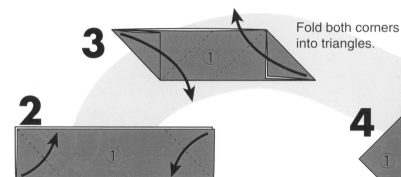

3 Fold both corners into triangles.

2

Fold both corners into triangles.

4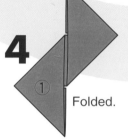

①

Folded.

1

①

Make a crease.

3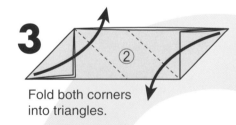

②

Fold both corners into triangles.

1

②

Make a crease.

2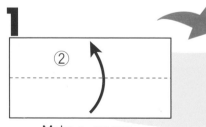

②

Fold both corners in opposite direction of ①.

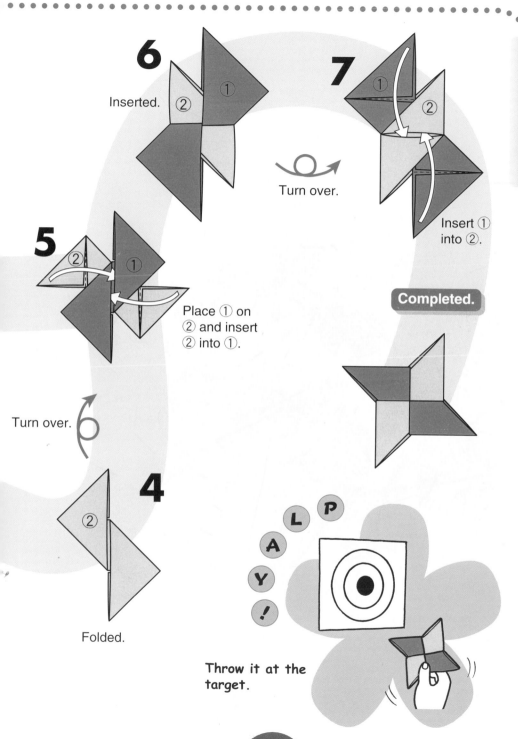

6

Inserted. ② ①

7 ① ②

Turn over.

Insert ① into ②.

Completed.

5 ② ①

Place ① on ② and insert ② into ①.

Turn over.

4 ②

Folded.

A L P Y !

Throw it at the target.

Top

★ You can place the flat origami on the ground and try to turn it over by throwing another one.

Paper 2 pieces of different color

1

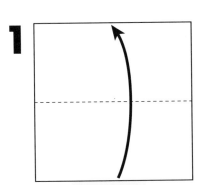

Make a crease.

2

Fold both corners into triangles.

Shift.

3

Make creases.

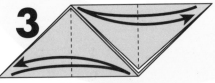

5

Put it on the other.

4

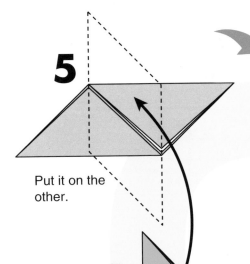

Fold another one in the same way.

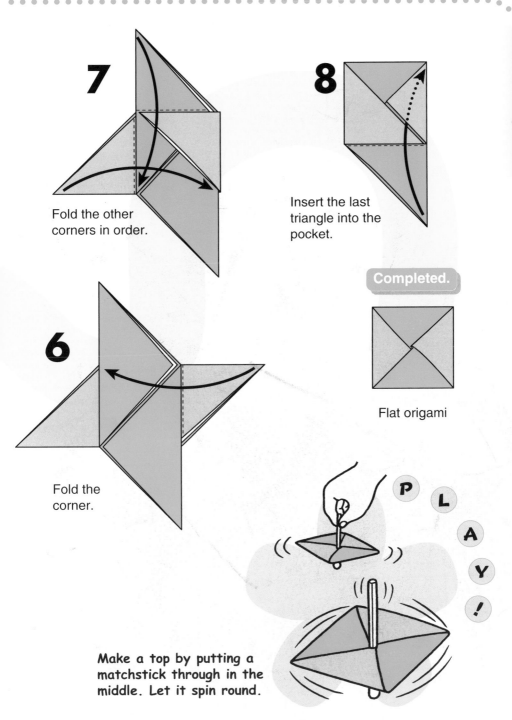

7

Fold the other corners in order.

8

Insert the last triangle into the pocket.

Completed.

Flat origami

6

Fold the corner.

P L A Y !

Make a top by putting a matchstick through in the middle. Let it spin round.

Camera

Paper | **Any color**

2

Folded.

1

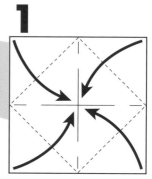

Make creases and fold four corners to center.

Turn over.

3

Fold four corners to center.

4

Folded.

Turn over.

5

Make creases.

Turn over.

6

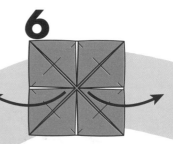

Unfold to the left and right.

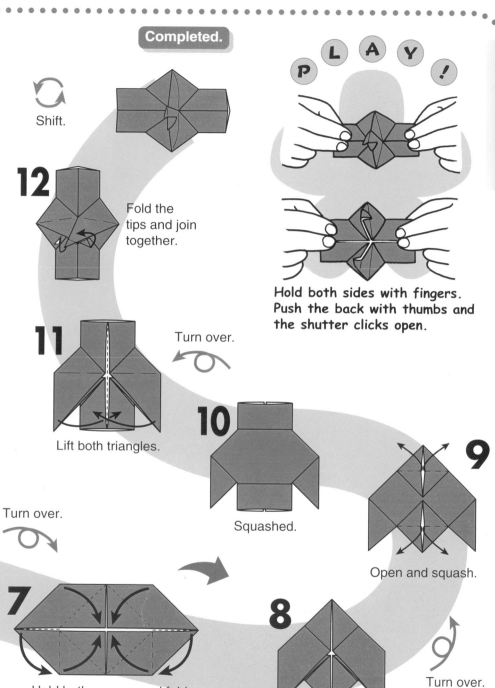

Completed.

PLAY!

Shift.

12 Fold the tips and join together.

Hold both sides with fingers. Push the back with thumbs and the shutter clicks open.

11 Lift both triangles.

Turn over.

10 Squashed.

9 Open and squash.

Turn over.

7 Hold both corners and fold on creases.

8 Folded.

Turn over.

25

Jumping frog

Paper | **Green or brown**

1

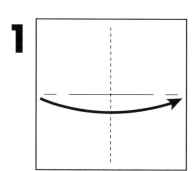

First make a horizontal crease and then fold in half vertically.

2

Make a crease by bringing the edge downward to the crease.

Turn over.

3

Make creases diagonally.

4

Fold on creases and squash.

Under the triangle, fold both sides to center.

6

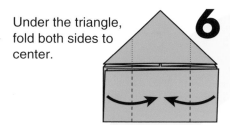

5

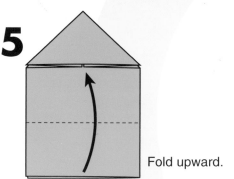

Fold upward.

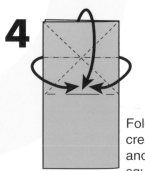

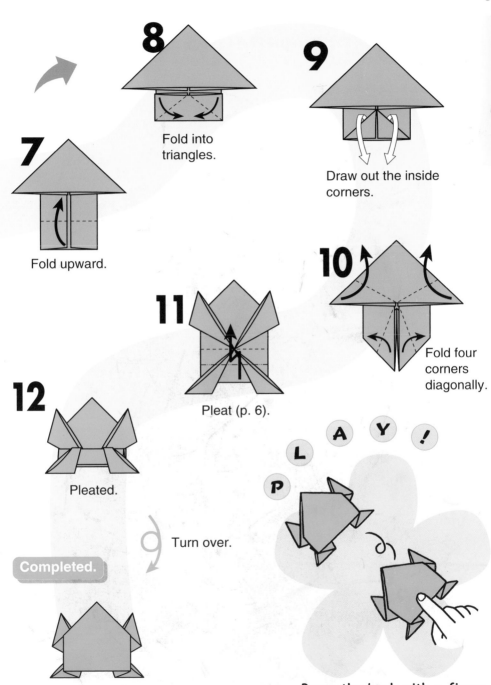

8

Fold into triangles.

9

Draw out the inside corners.

7

Fold upward.

10

Fold four corners diagonally.

11

Pleat (p. 6).

12

Pleated.

Turn over.

Completed.

P L A Y !

Press the back with a finger and slide it off and the frog jumps.

Carp streamer

Paper Red or violet blue or black

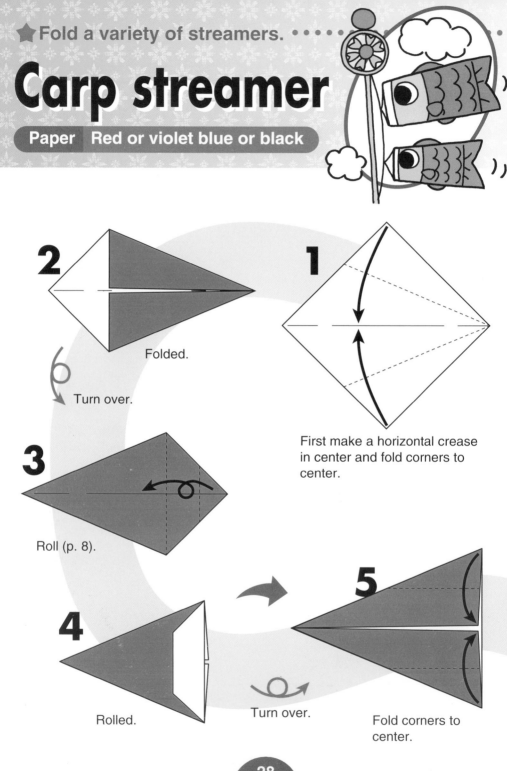

2

Folded.

Turn over.

1

First make a horizontal crease in center and fold corners to center.

3

Roll (p. 8).

4

Rolled.

Turn over.

5

Fold corners to center.

10

Folded.

Turn over.

Completed.

9

Fold diagonally.

8

Inside reverse fold.

7

Inside reverse fold (p. 7).

6

Fold upward and insert the corner into the above pocket.

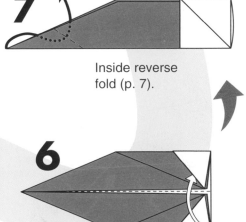

P L A Y !

Draw a large eye and scales. Paste the models on drawing paper as if fluttering.

Hina dolls

Paper **Red, violet blue, etc.**

1

Fold in half.

2

Fold only the upper layer.

3

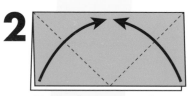

Fold so that the tip comes out a little.

4

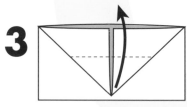

Fold and cover the triangle.

6   **Empress**

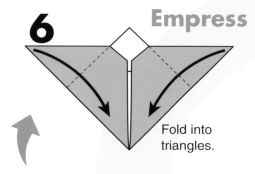

Fold into triangles.

5

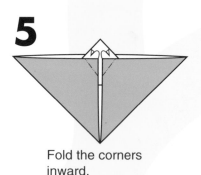

Fold the corners inward.

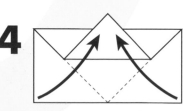

8

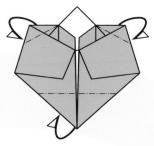

Completed.

7

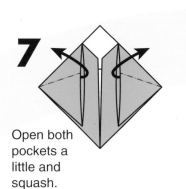

Open both pockets a little and squash.

Fold each corner to the reverse side.

Emperor

6

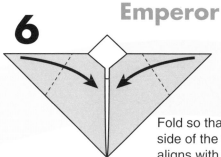

Fold so that the side of the triangle aligns with the center.

7

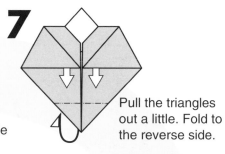

Pull the triangles out a little. Fold to the reverse side.

Completed.

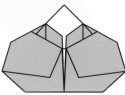

A L P Y !

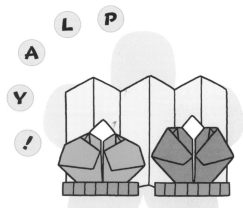

Paste golden paper on a cardboard and make a gilded folding screen.

Bill

Paper | **Any color**

Begin with step 4 of Camera on page 24.

1

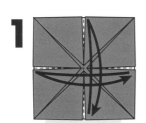

Make creases in half.

Turn over.

2

Make a crease horizontally.

3

Make a crease vertically.

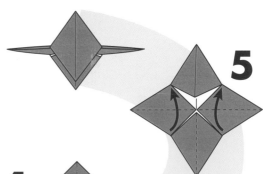

PLAY!

Move wings sideways. The bill opens and closes.

Completed.

5

Folding.

4

Pull out the top flap and fold in half.

Part 2 Living Things

From your favorite animals
to lovely flowers !

Ladybird

Paper Red

1

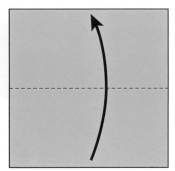

Fold in half.

2

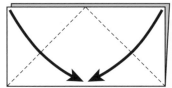

Fold into triangles.

3

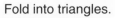

Folded.

 Turn over.

4

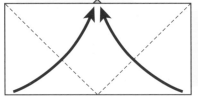

Fold into triangles.

5

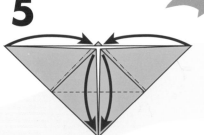

Bring each corner downward
to the bottom corner and
squash both sides.

Completed.

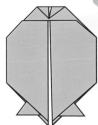

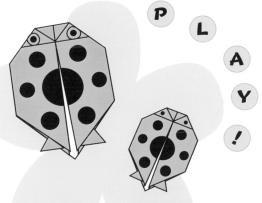

P L A Y !

Draw black dots on the back with a marker.

9

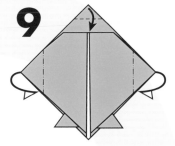

Fold the top corner into a triangle and fold both sides backward.

8

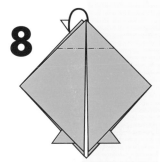

Fold the upper corner into a triangle backward.

6

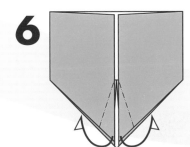

Fold each corner backward.

7

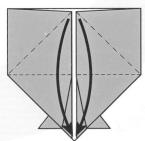

Bring each corner downward to the bottom corner and squash both sides.

Cicada

| Paper | Gray or dark brown transparent paper |

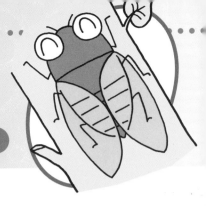

1

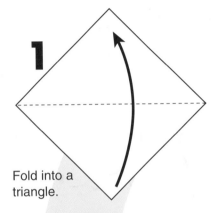

Fold into a triangle.

2

Bring both corners to the top corner.

3

Fold a small triangle.

4

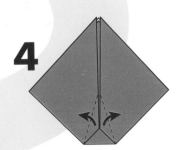

Open the upper flaps and squash.

5

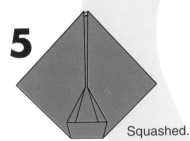

Squashed.

Turn over.

6

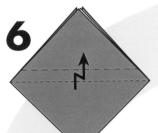

The two layers together (p. 6).

36

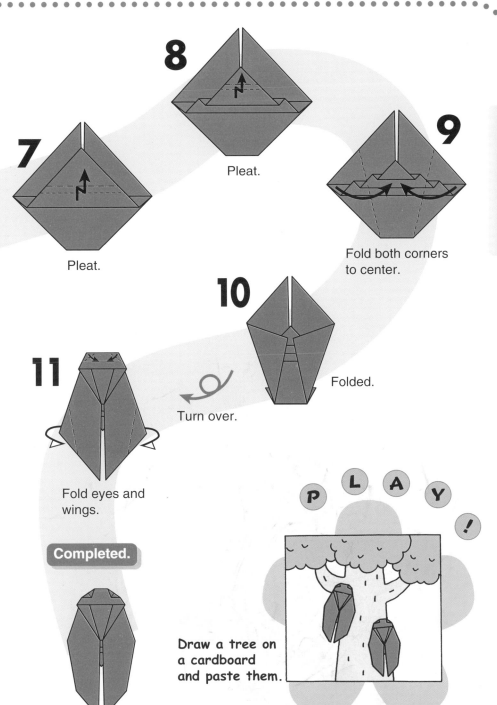

8

Pleat.

7

Pleat.

9

Fold both corners to center.

10

Folded.

Turn over.

11

Fold eyes and wings.

Completed.

PLAY!

Draw a tree on a cardboard and paste them.

Stag beetle

Paper | **Dark brown or black**

2 Turn over.

Make a vertical crease and fold into a triangle.

1

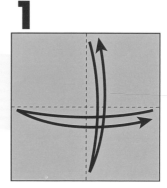

Make creases.

3

Hold both corners and fold on creases.

5

Fold both corners backward.

4

Fold both corners downward.

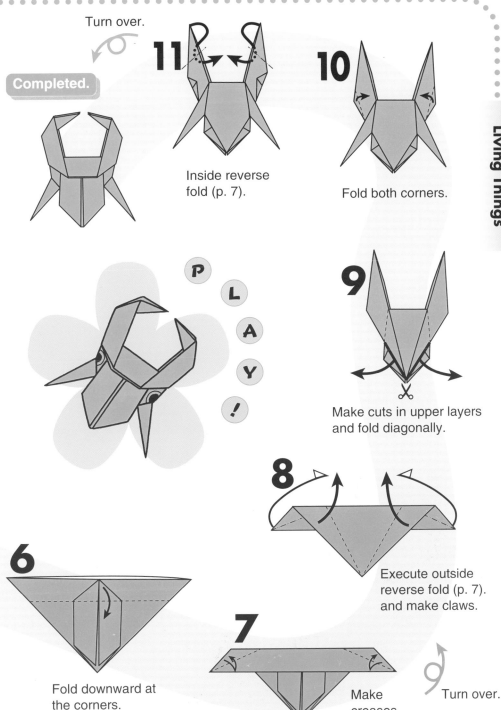

Turn over.

Completed.

11 Inside reverse fold (p. 7).

10 Fold both corners.

P
L
A
Y
!

9 Make cuts in upper layers and fold diagonally.

8 Execute outside reverse fold (p. 7). and make claws.

6 Fold downward at the corners.

7 Make creases.

Turn over.

39

Butterfly

Paper **Any color**

2

Fold in half.

1

First make horizontal and vertical creases and fold both edges to center.

3

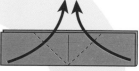

Fold upward.

Turn over.

4

Folded.

5

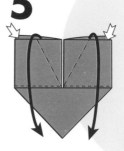

Open and squash.

Completed.

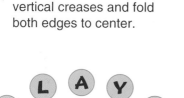

Draw patterns on the wings.

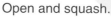

Parakeet

Paper   Any color

1

Make triangle creases.

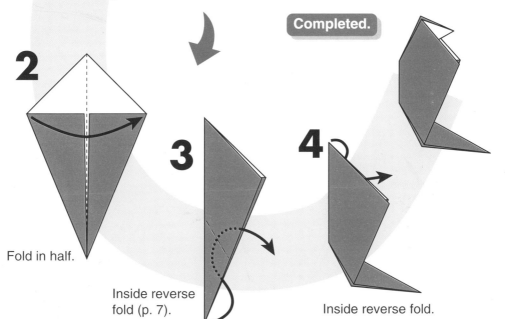

Draw a perch and paste it.

P
L
A
Y
!

Completed.

2

Fold in half.

3

Inside reverse fold (p. 7).

4

Inside reverse fold.

Pigeon

Paper | **White or gray**

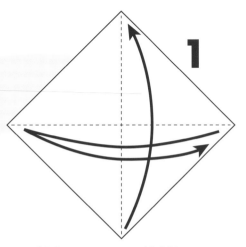

1

Make creases and fold into a triangle.

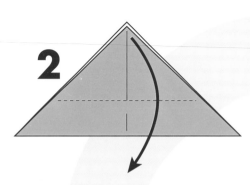

2

Fold the upper layer so that the tip sticks out of the edge a little.

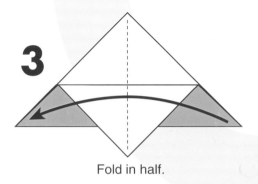

3

Fold in half.

Shift.

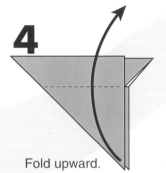

4

Fold upward.

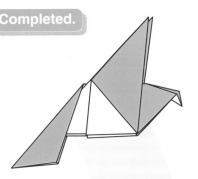

P L A Y !

Paint in lovely eyes and
draw wings.

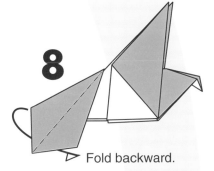

8

Fold backward.

7

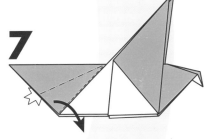

Open and squash.

5

Fold backward.

6

Inside reverse
fold (p. 7)

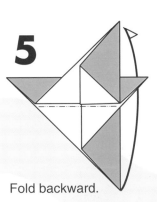

Crane

Paper | **Any color**

1

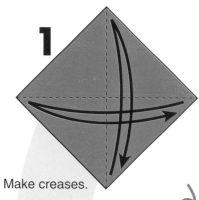

Make creases.

Turn over.

2

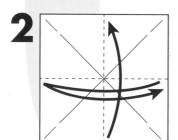

Make a vertical crease and fold in half.

3

Pinch both corners, fold on creases and squash.

5

Spread out on creases and squash.

4

Make creases. Repeat on the other side.

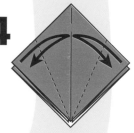 Shift.

6

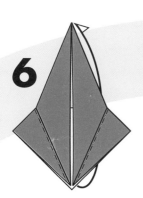

Spread out. Repeat on the other side.

7

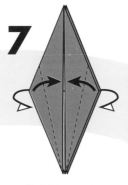

Fold to center. Repeat on the other side.

8

Inside reverse fold (p. 7)

9

Inside reverse fold.

10

Folded.

11

Pull out wings sideways and raise the back.

Completed.

P L A Y !

Use double size of paper cut in the middle.
You can make cranes joined together.

Goldfish & Helmet

Paper	Red or black

1

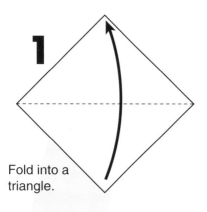

Fold into a triangle.

6

Turn over.

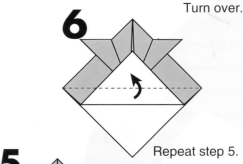

Repeat step 5.

5

Fold the upper flap upward.

2

Bring both corners to the top corner.

3

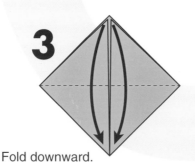

Fold downward.

Shift.

4

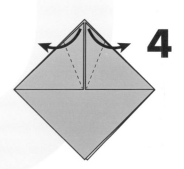

Fold diagonally.

Goldfish

7

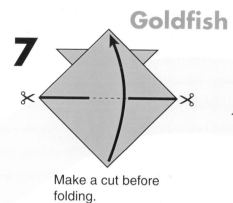

Make a cut before folding.

8

Insert a finger and open. Squash.

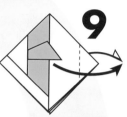

Outside reverse fold on the crease from the cut. (p. 7)

9

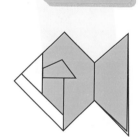

Helmet

Turn over.

7

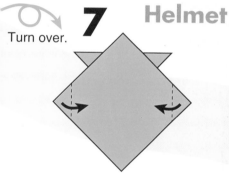

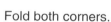

Fold both corners.

8

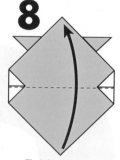

Fold upward.

Completed.

9

Folded.

Completed.

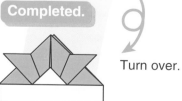

Turn over.

P L A Y !

Use a large sheet of paper like a newspaper.
You can put it on.

P L A Y !

Make a mobile with helmets and goldfishes.

47

Squid

Paper | **White or pale yellow**

2

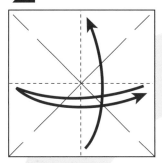

Make a vertical crease
and fold in half.

1

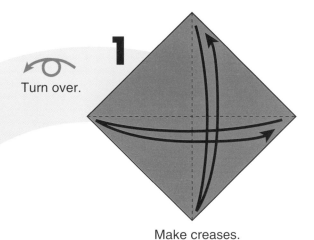

Turn over.

Make creases.

3

Pinch both corners, fold
on creases and squash.

4

Folding.

5

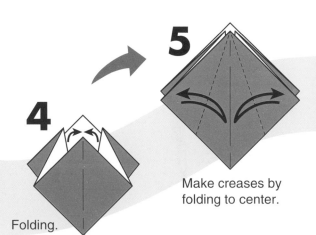

Make creases by
folding to center.

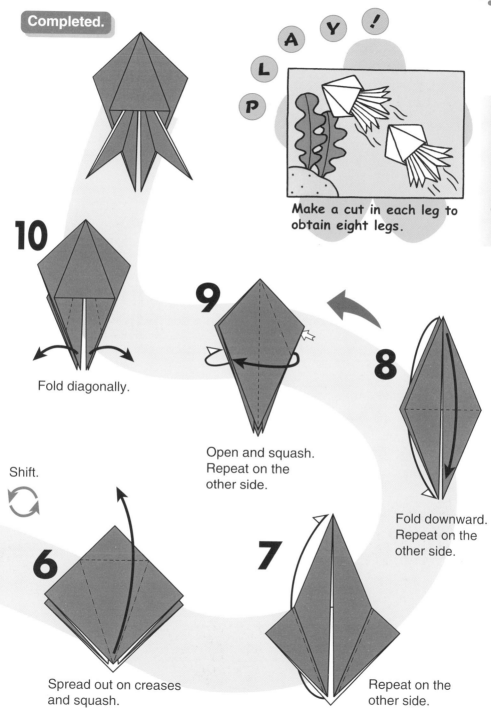

Completed.

P L A Y !

Make a cut in each leg to obtain eight legs.

Living Things

10

Fold diagonally.

9

Open and squash.
Repeat on the
other side.

8

Fold downward.
Repeat on the
other side.

Shift.

6

Spread out on creases
and squash.

7

Repeat on the
other side.

49

⭐ Be careful not to be nipped with its claws. • • • • • •

Crab

Paper | **Red or orange or green**

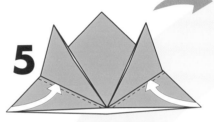

1

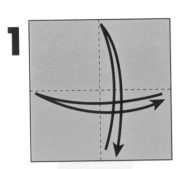

Make creases.

5

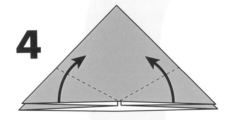

Fold under the upper flaps.

Turn over.

2

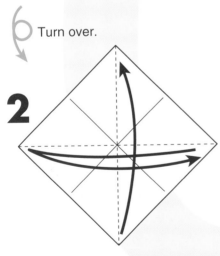

Make a vertical crease and fold into a triangle.

4

Fold diagonally.

3

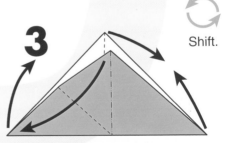

Shift.

Pinch both corners and fold in the direction of arrows.

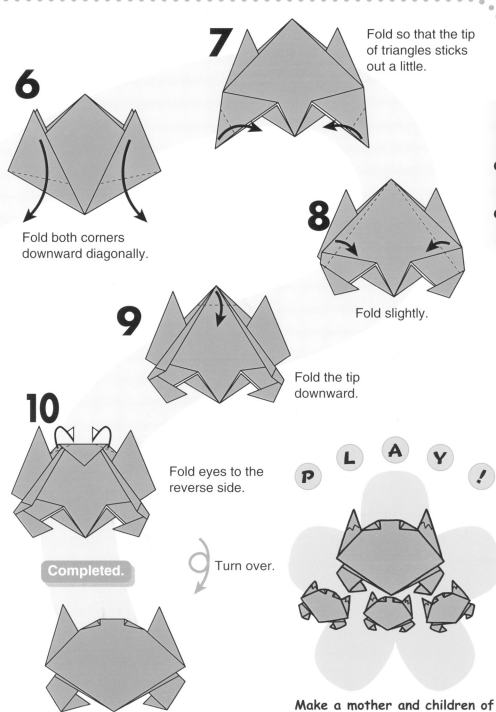

6

Fold both corners downward diagonally.

7 Fold so that the tip of triangles sticks out a little.

8 Fold slightly.

9 Fold the tip downward.

10 Fold eyes to the reverse side.

Completed.

Turn over.

P L A Y !

Make a mother and children of crabs and paint in the claws.

Turtle

Paper | **Green or yellowish green**

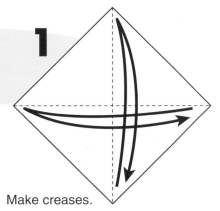

1

Make creases.

2

Fold each corner to center.

↺ Shift.

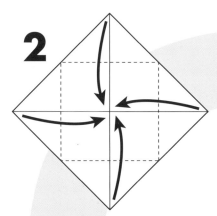

3

Fold both corners into triangles.

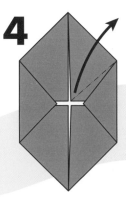

4

Pull out the corner.

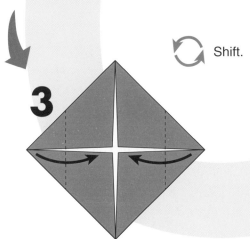

7

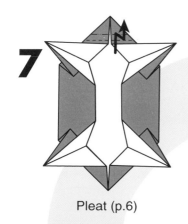

Pleat (p.6)

8

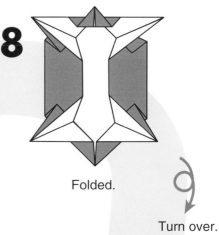

Folded.

Turn over.

Completed.

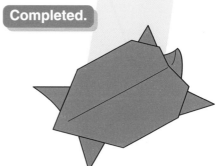

6

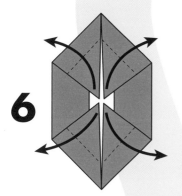

Lift each corner, fold twisting and squash.

5

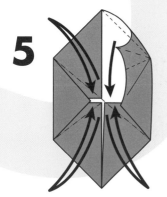

Fold and squash over the flap. Fold the other corners in the same way.

P L A Y !

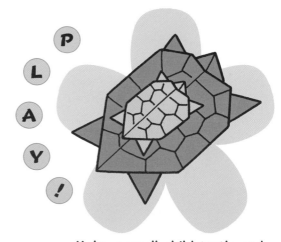

Make a small child turtle and put it on a large parent turtle.

Spiral shell

Paper | **Any color**

1

Make horizontal and vertical creases and fold the right corner to center.

2

Fold in half.

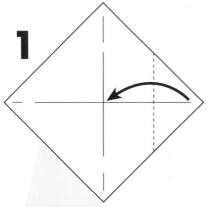

3

Open and squash.

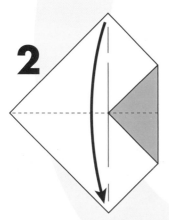

4

Fold the back triangle.

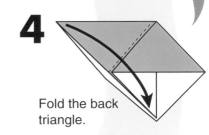

5

Fold the triangle inward.

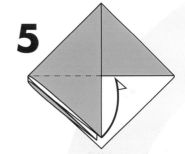

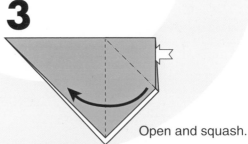

54

6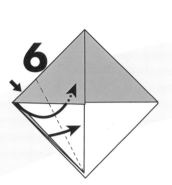

Make an inside reverse fold (p. 7) so that the edge align with the center.

7 Pleat (p. 6)

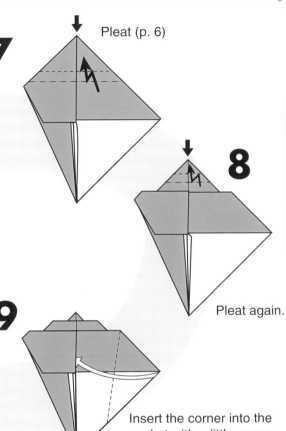

8

Pleat again.

9

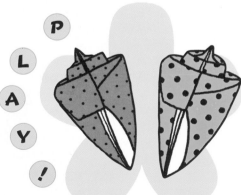

Insert the corner into the pocket with a little space left near the bottom.

10

Insert a finger and let it bulge in a rounded shape.

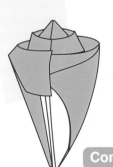

Completed.

P
L
A
Y
!

If you use paper with colored patterns, you can make lovely spiral shells.

Dolphin

Paper | **Light blue**

1

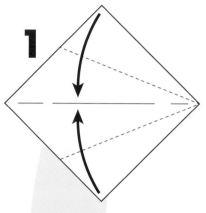

First make a horizontal crease in center and fold corners to center.

5

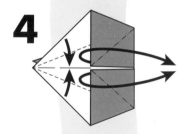

Fold sideways.

4

Open and squash.

2

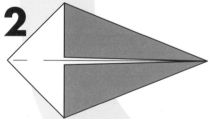

Folded.

Turn over.

3

Fold so that both corners meet.

7

Turn back.

6

Fold the corner to center.

8

Fold in half.

10

Inside reverse fold (p. 7)

9

Fold so that edges become vertcal.

11

Turn back the lower flap.

Completed.

P L A Y !

Put a small balloon (p.14) on the head and arrange with the fur seal (p.58) side by side.

⭐ It likes to play with a ball. • • • • • • • • • •

Fur seal

Paper **Gray**

1

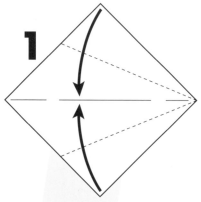

First make a horizontal crease in center and fold corners to center.

2

Fold backward so that corners meet.

3

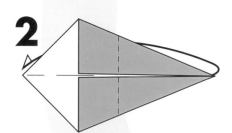

Open and squash.

4

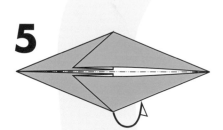

Turn back the lower flap.

5

Fold in half backwad.

6

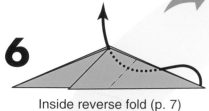

Inside reverse fold (p. 7)

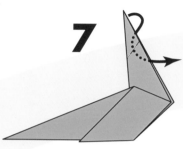

7

Inside reverse fold.

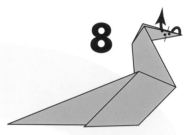

8

Inside reverse fold.

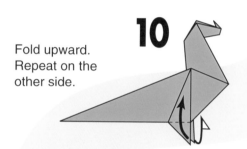

10

Fold upward.
Repeat on the
other side.

9

Fold so that edges become
vertical.

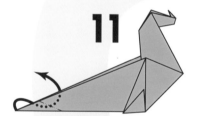

11

Inside reverse fold.

Completed.

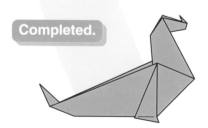

P L A Y !

Make a small balloon (p.14)
and put on the head.

Whale

Paper | **Red or black**

2

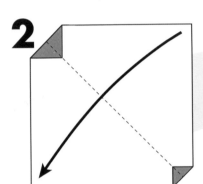

Fold in half.

1

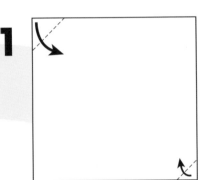

Fold two triangles of different size.

3

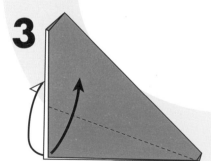

Fold diagonally. Repeat on the other side.

4

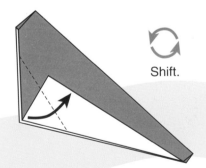

Shift.

Fold so that edges align. Repeat on the other side.

8

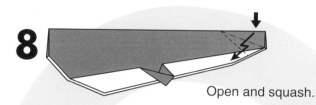

Open and squash.

7

Fold into a small triangle. Repeat on the other side.

Completed.

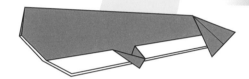

6

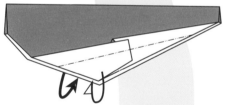

Fold inward. Repeat on the other side.

5

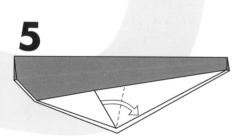

Pull out the triangle.

Paste the whale on the drawing of the ocean and let it blow.

Sunfish

Paper **Light blue or brown**

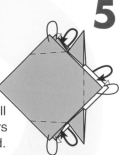

1

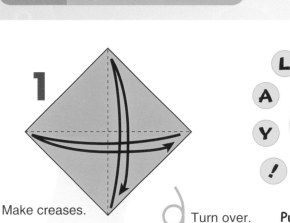

Make creases.

Turn over.

L A Y P !

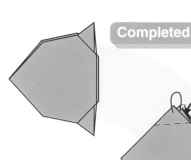

→

Push the corner in to make a small mouth.

2

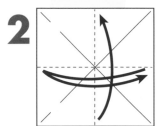

Make a vertical crease
and fold in half.

Completed.

5

Fold all
corners
inward.

Shift.

3

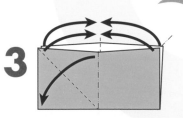

Pinch both corners, fold
on creases and squash.

4

Make inside reverse folds
(p. 7) and pull out triangles.

Horse

Paper | **Brown or white**

1

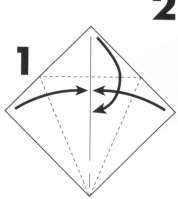

Make triangle creases and fold on them.

2

Open the bottom corner and squash.

3

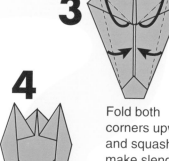

Fold both corners upward and squash to make slender ears.

4

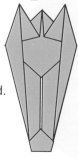

Folded.

Turn over.

5

Fold top and bottom.

Completed.

P L A Y !

Paste the face on drawing paper and paint the body.

Dog and Cat

| Paper | Any color |

Face

2

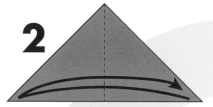

Fold and unfold.

1

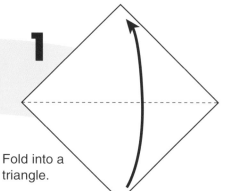

Fold into a triangle.

3

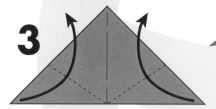

Fold corners diagonally.

4

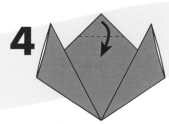

Fold the upper layer into a triangle.

↻ Shift.

4

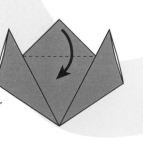

Fold the two layers together into a triangle.

5

Folded.

Body

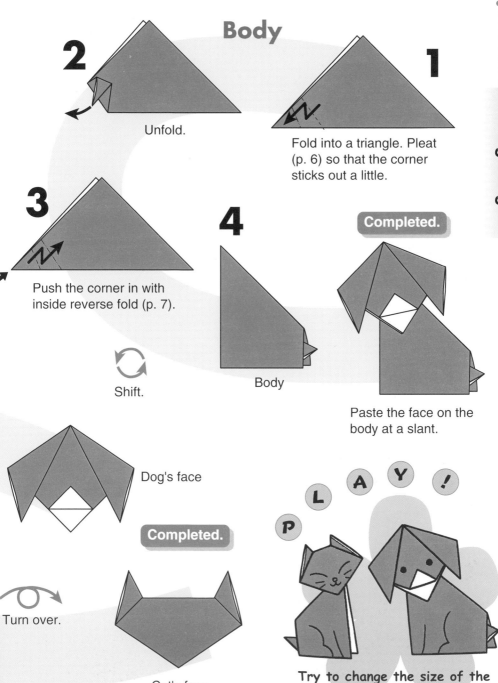

2

Unfold.

1

Fold into a triangle. Pleat
(p. 6) so that the corner
sticks out a little.

3

Push the corner in with
inside reverse fold (p. 7).

Shift.

4

Body

Completed.

Paste the face on the
body at a slant.

Dog's face

Turn over.

Completed.

Cat's face

P L A Y !

Try to change the size of the
body, bigger or smaller.

Rabbit

Paper **Red or pink or brown**

1

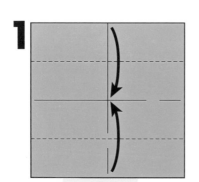

Make cross creases and fold edges to center.

2

Fold to center.

3

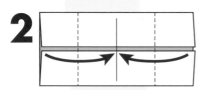

Open and squash.

4

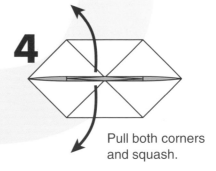

Pull both corners and squash.

5

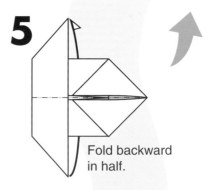

Fold backward in half.

6

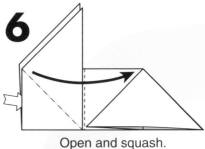

Open and squash.

8 Fold.

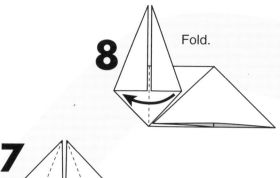

9

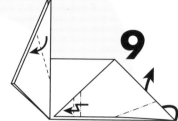

Ears: Fold only the upper flap.
Legs: Pleat (p. 6)
Tail: Inside reverse fold (p. 7)

7

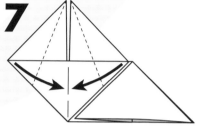

Fold to center.

10

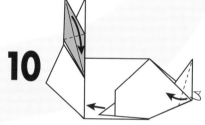

Ears: Fold downard.
Legs: Unfold.
Tail: Fold in half.

11

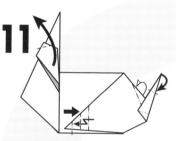

Ears: Fold upward a little.
Legs: Inside reverse fold.
Tail: Fold inward.
Fold the other side in the
same way as steps 9-11.

Completed.

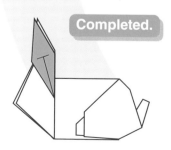

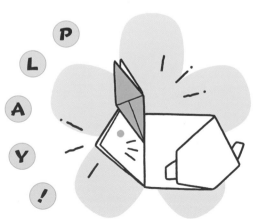

P
L
A
Y
!

Paint in whiskers and red eyes.

⭐ It has a lovely tail. • • • • • • • • • • • • • •

Pig

Paper | Pink or flesh color

2

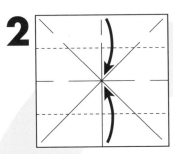

Fold on creases.

1

Make creases.

3

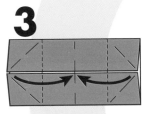

Fold edges to center.

Turn over.

6

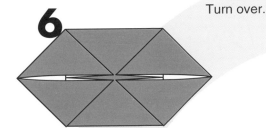

Squashed.

4

Open and squash.

5

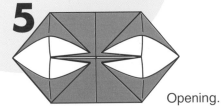

Opening.

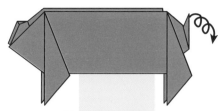

Completed.

Twist the tail.

P L A Y !

Paint in eys and hoofs.

11

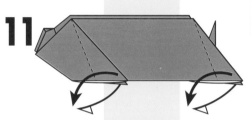

Fold diagonally and repeat on the on the side.

7

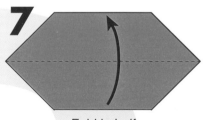

Fold in half.

10

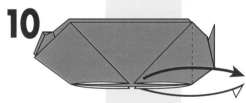

Fold and repeat on the other side.

8

Inside reverse fold (p. 7)

9

Inside reverse fold.

Living Things

Cow

| Paper | White or brown |

Face

1

Make creases.

2

Make a vertical crease and fold in half.

Turn over.

3

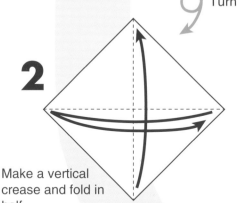

Fold on creases.

4

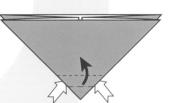

Open both sides and squash.

5

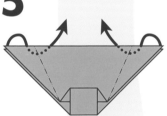

Inside reverse fold (p. 7)

6

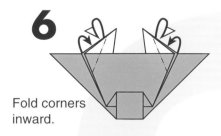

Fold corners inward.

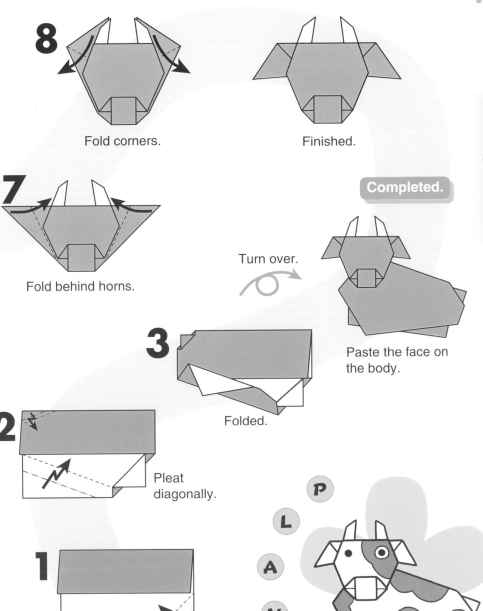

8

Fold corners.

Finished.

7

Fold behind horns.

Completed.

Turn over.

Paste the face on the body.

3

Folded.

2

Pleat diagonally.

1

Fold down 1/3 from the edge.
Pleat (p. 6) one corner.

Body

P
L
A
Y
!

Paint in eyes and draw patterns of the body.

Koala

`Paper` `Brown`

Face

1

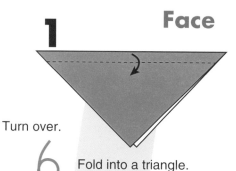

Turn over.

Fold into a triangle.
Fold down about 1/8
form the edge.

7

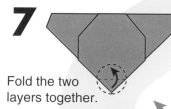

Fold the two
layers together.

Turn over.

6

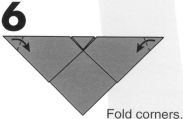

Fold corners.

2

Fold so that both corners meet
the bottom corner.

5

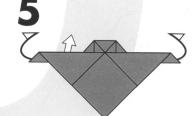

Pull out both
corners.

3

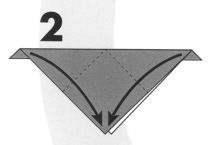

Fold corners into
triangles of the
same size.

4

Fold diagonally.

72

Steps 8-10 show part of the face.

9
Fold inward.

10
Fold backward.

11
Finished.

Completed.

8
Fold diagonally.

5
Body

Paste the face on the body.

4
Fold in half.

3
Unfold and squash.

P
L
A
Y
!

For the child koala, use paper 1/4 the size of original paper.

Inside reverse fold (p.7)

Let's make parent and child koalas.

2
Fold so that corners meet the crease.

Turn over.

1
Fold in half and fold back, leaving a little space.

Body

Panda

Paper | **Black**

2

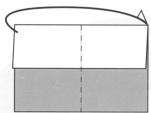

Fold in half backward.

1

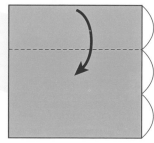

Fold down 1/3 from the edge.

3

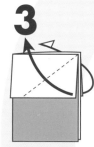

Fold diagonally, leaving space 1 cm from the edge. Repeat on the other side.

4

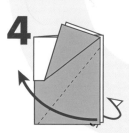

Fold, leaving space 1 cm from the top corner and 5mm from the bottom corner. Repeat on the other side.

5

Fold so that edges align. Repeat on the other side.

6

Open.

Completed.

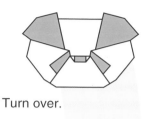

Turn over.

P L A Y !

12

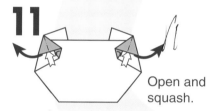

Fold bottom corners.

Fold down 1/5 from the edge. Fold bottom corners diagonally. Fold in half backward.

11

Open and squash.

10

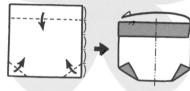

Folded.

9

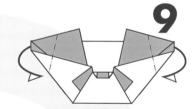

Fold ears backward.

Turn over.

7

Fold so that the bottom edge aligns with triangle corners.

8

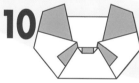

Fold a little.

75

Giraffe

Paper **Yellow**

1

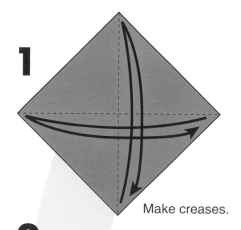

Make creases.

2

Make a vertical crease
and fold in half.

Turn over.

3

Pinch both
corners, fold on
creases and
squash.

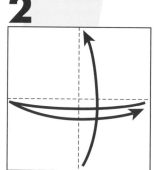

5

Open and
squash.

4

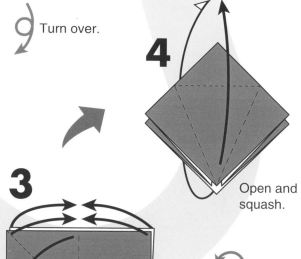

Open and
squash.

Shift.

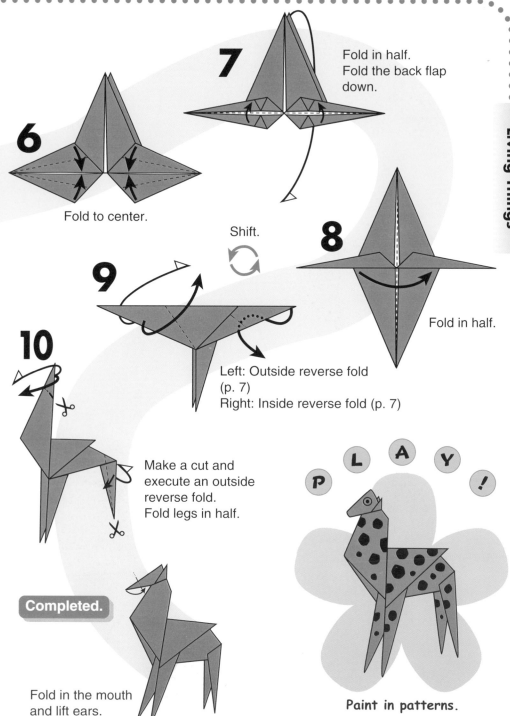

6 Fold to center.

7 Fold in half.
Fold the back flap down.

Shift.

8 Fold in half.

9 Left: Outside reverse fold (p. 7)
Right: Inside reverse fold (p. 7)

10 Make a cut and execute an outside reverse fold.
Fold legs in half.

Completed.

Fold in the mouth and lift ears.

P L A Y !

Paint in patterns.

Elephant

Paper **Gray**

Body

1

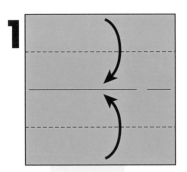

Make a crease in center and fold edges to center.

6

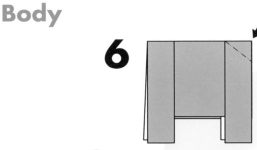

Inside reverse fold (p. 7)

2

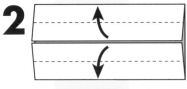

Fold backward.

Shift.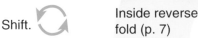

5

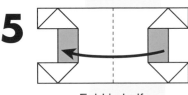

Fold in half.

3

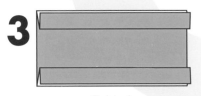

Folded.

Turn over.

4

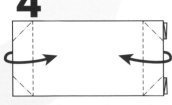

Open flaps and squash corners.

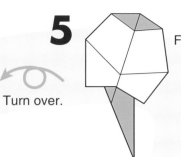
Folded.

5

Turn over.

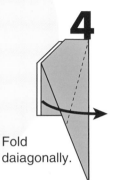

4

Fold daiagonally.

Completed.

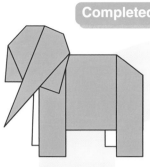

Paste the face on the body.

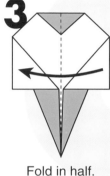

3

Fold in half.

2

Fold so that each corner sticks out of edges.

7

Finished.

Face

1

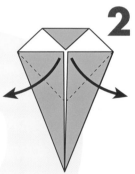

The paper size is 1/4 of that of the body.

Fold each corner into a triangle.

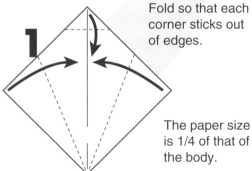

P L A Y !

Draw eyes, wrinkles and toenails.

Living Things

Lion

Paper | **Yellow or brown**

2

Turn over.

Folded.

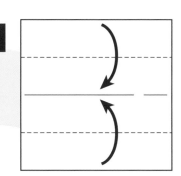

1

Make a crease in center and fold edges to center.

3

Fold in half and unfold.

4

Fold the edge to center and fold backward. (Pleat: p. 6)

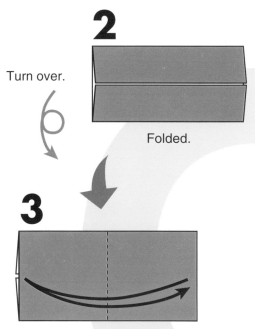

5

Fold on the crease.

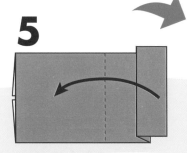

Completed.

Draw the face and mane.

10

Fold the tail sideways.

9

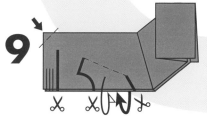

Cut along thick lines. Fold the belly inward. Push the back in.

8

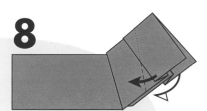

Pull up the face.

6

Fold diagonally.

7

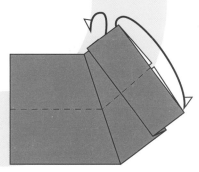

Fold in half on the crease.

Tiger

Paper **Yellow**

2

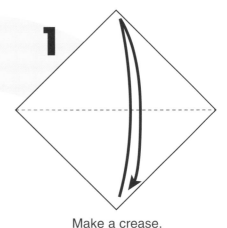

Fold diagonally.

1

Make a crease.

3

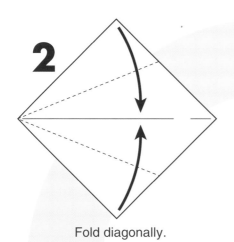

Fold the triangle
in half.

5

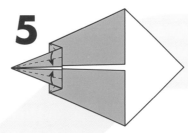

Fold to center and squash.

4

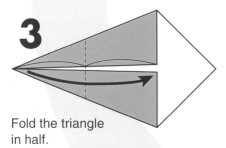

Fold on a crease about 2cm
from the edge.

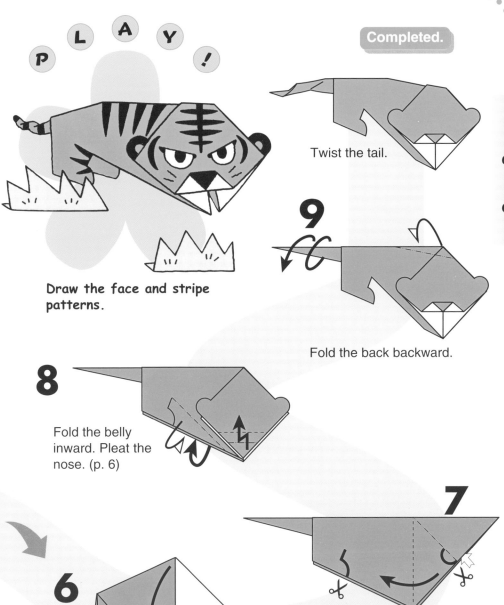

P L A Y !

Completed.

Twist the tail.

Draw the face and stripe patterns.

9

Fold the back backward.

8

Fold the belly inward. Pleat the nose. (p. 6)

7

Cut along thick lines. Open and squash.

6

Fold the whole in half.

Crocodile

Paper	Green or brown

Head

2

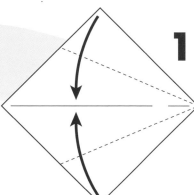

Fold in half
backward.

1

Make a crease in center
and fold diagonally.

3

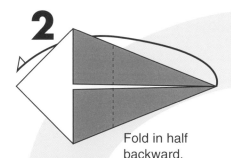

Open and
squash.

6

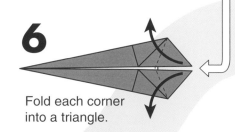

Fold each corner
into a triangle.

4

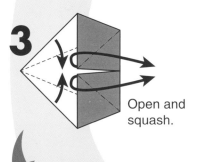

Open both sides
and squash the
triangles.

5

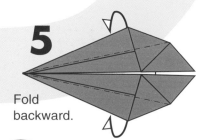

Fold
backward.

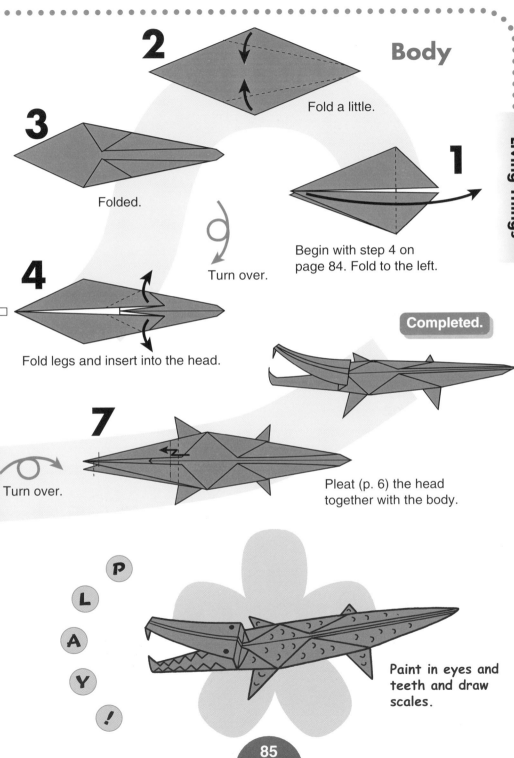

2

Fold a little.

Body

3

Folded.

Turn over.

1

Begin with step 4 on page 84. Fold to the left.

4

Fold legs and insert into the head.

Completed.

7

Turn over.

Pleat (p. 6) the head together with the body.

P L A Y !

Paint in eyes and teeth and draw scales.

Living Things

Tyrannosaurus

Paper **Brown**

1

Make creases.

Turn over.

2

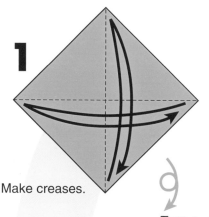

Make a vertical crease
and fold in half.

3

Pinch both corners, fold
on creases and squash.

4

Open and
squash.

5

Repeat on the
other side.

Fold up the
upper flap.

6

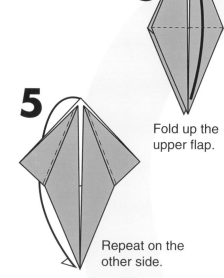

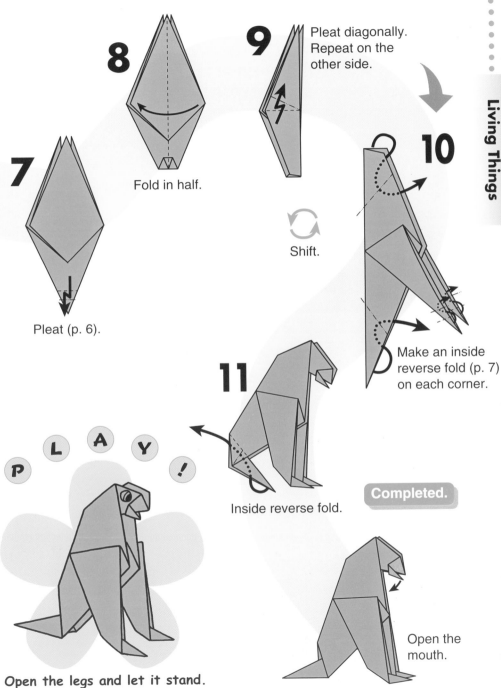

7

Pleat (p. 6).

8

Fold in half.

9

Pleat diagonally. Repeat on the other side.

Shift.

10

Make an inside reverse fold (p. 7) on each corner.

11

Inside reverse fold.

Completed.

Open the mouth.

P L A Y !

Open the legs and let it stand.

Diplodocus

Paper	Dark brown or ocher

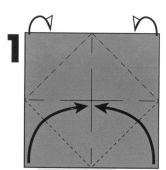

1

Make cross creases.
Upper corners: mountain fold.
Bottom corners: valley fold.

2

Fold so that edges align.

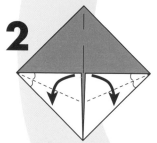

3

Inside reverse fold (p. 7)

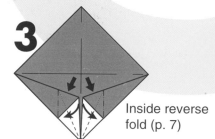

6

Pull down the middle corners and squash.

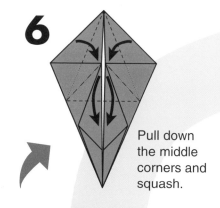

5

Fold to center.

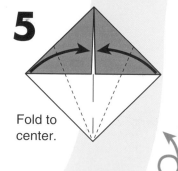

Turn over.

4

Folded.

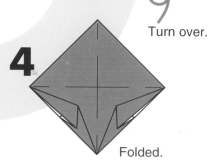

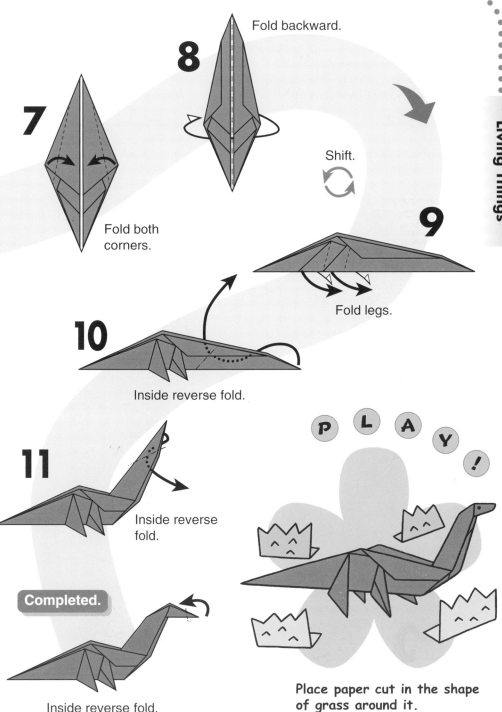

Fold backward.

8

7

Fold both corners.

Shift.

9

Fold legs.

10

Inside reverse fold.

11

Inside reverse fold.

Completed.

Inside reverse fold.

P L A Y !

Place paper cut in the shape of grass around it.

Tulip

Paper | **Green or any other color**

Flower

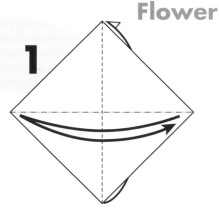

1

Make a vertical crease and fold backward.

2

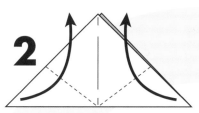

Fold corners diagonally.

3

Folded. Unfold.

4

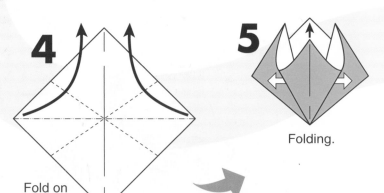

Fold on creases.

5

Folding.

Leaves

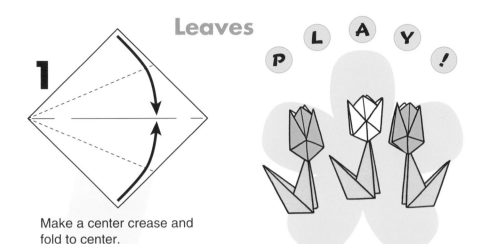

1

Make a center crease and fold to center.

Using paper of various color, fold a lot of tulips and make a flower garden.

2

Fold to center.

3

Fold in half and make an inside reverse fold.

4 Finished.

Completed.

6

Fold corners to center. Repeat on the other side.

7

Completed.

Make a hole at the bottom of the flower and insert the leaves.

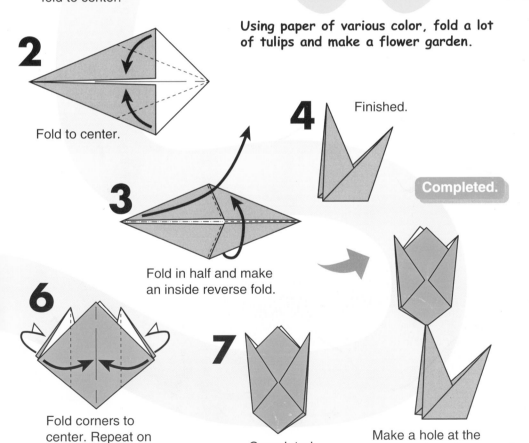

Rose

Paper | **Red, pink or yellow**

1

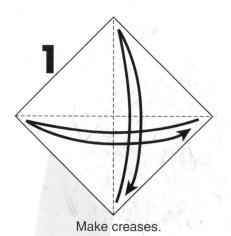

Make creases.

2

Fold each corner to center.

3

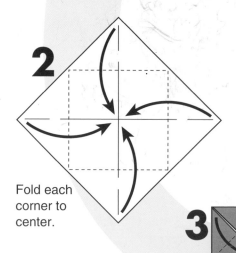

Fold each corner to center.

4

Fold each corner to center.

5

Folded.

Turn over.

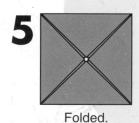

Shift.

6

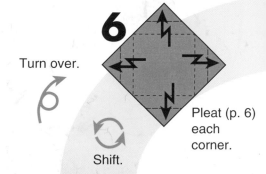

Pleat (p. 6) each corner.

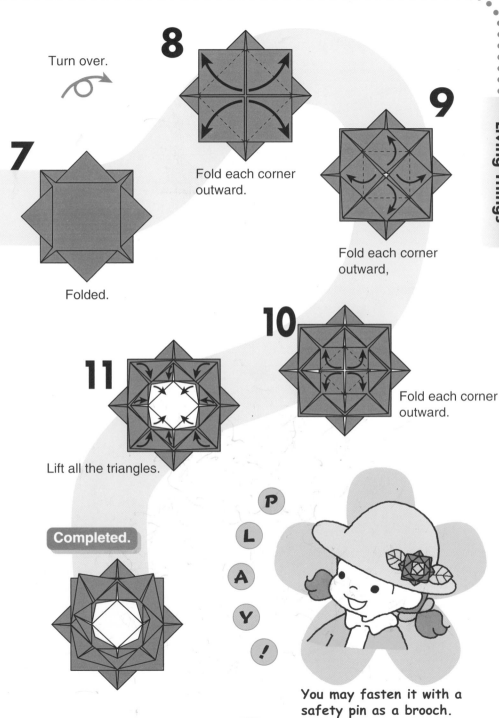

Turn over.

8

Fold each corner outward.

7

Folded.

9

Fold each corner outward,

11

Lift all the triangles.

10

Fold each corner outward.

Completed.

P
L
A
Y
!

You may fasten it with a safety pin as a brooch.

Morning glory

Paper   **Red, blue or green**

Flower

1

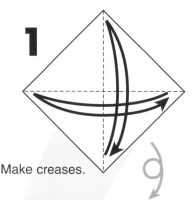

Make creases.

Turn over.

6

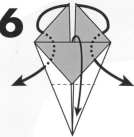

Open and squash.

5

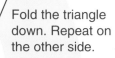

Fold the triangle down. Repeat on the other side.

2

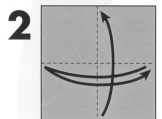

Make a vertical crease and fold in half.

3

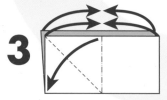

Pinch both corners, fold on creases and squash.

4

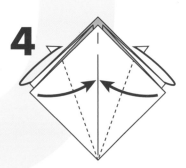

Fold to center. Repeat on the other side.

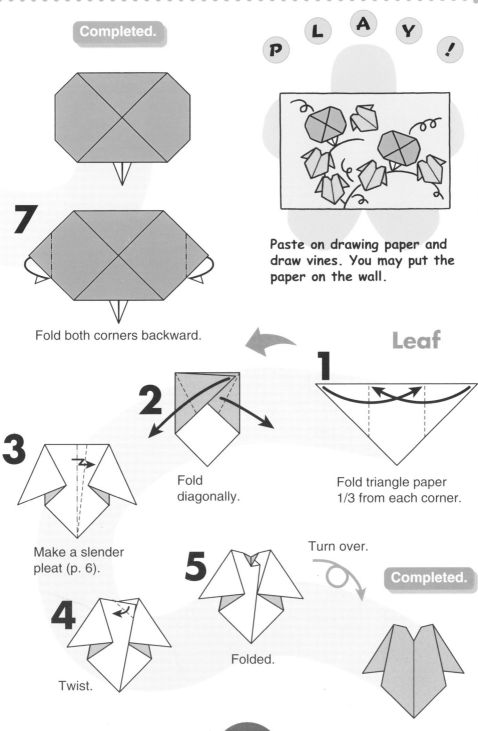

Completed.

Living Things

Paste on drawing paper and draw vines. You may put the paper on the wall.

7

Fold both corners backward.

Leaf

1 Fold triangle paper 1/3 from each corner.

2 Fold diagonally.

3 Make a slender pleat (p. 6).

4 Twist.

5 Folded.

Turn over.

Completed.

95

★ Small flowers are lovely. ● ● ● ● ● ● ● ●

Hydrangea

Paper | **Light blue or pink**

1

Make creases.

Turn over.

2

Make a vertical crease and fold in half.

3

Pinch both corners, fold on creases and squash.

4

Folding.

5

Fold into a triangle.

6

Open and squash.

Completed.

P L A Y !

Make a lot of flowers with small paper and paste them on drawing paper.

Part 3

Furniture and Small Articles

Let's play house with origami.

Chair

Paper | Any color

2 Fold corners to center.

1 Make creases.

3 Folded.

4 Fold corners to center.

Turn over.

5 Folded.

Completed.

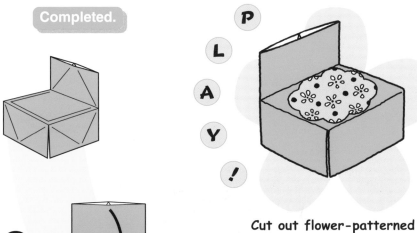

P L A Y !

Cut out flower-patterned paper and make a cushion.

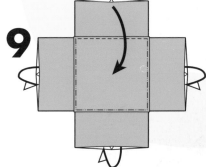

9

Valley fold one flap and mountain fold the others.

Turn over.

8

Open and squash.

6

Fold corners to center.

7

Folded.

Turn over.

Sofa

Paper | **Any color**

1

Fold in half.

2

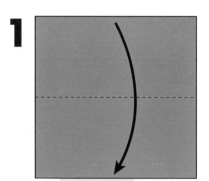

Fold the upper layer in half to make a crease. Fold the edge to the center crease.

3

Make a crease.

4

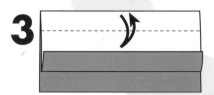

Fold so that the edges aligin.

5

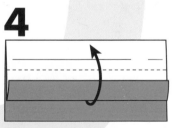

Fold backward in half.

6

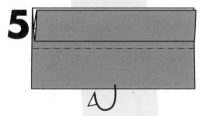

Open and squash.

7

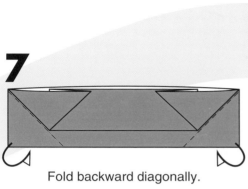

Fold backward diagonally.

8

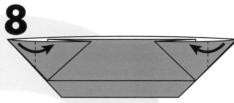

Fold each corner into a triangle 1/3 from the corner.

9

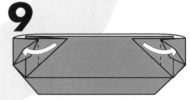

Fold 1/3 from each corner and insert into the pocket.

10

Shift.

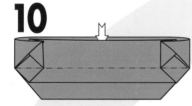

Pull the upper layer toward you and enlarge the bottom.

11

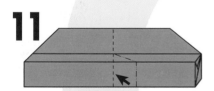

Fold the middle and bend.

Completed.

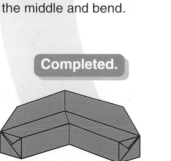

P L A Y !

Put together the long sofa and bent one.

Desk

Paper | **Any color**

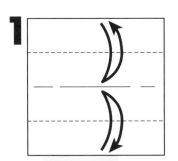

1

Make a crease in center
and fold edges to center.

5

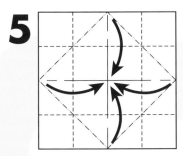

Fold all on creases.

4

Turn over.

Unfold.

2

Make creases in the
same way.

Turn over.

3

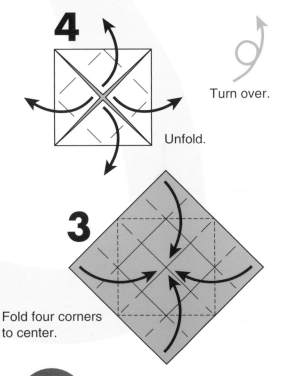

Fold four corners
to center.

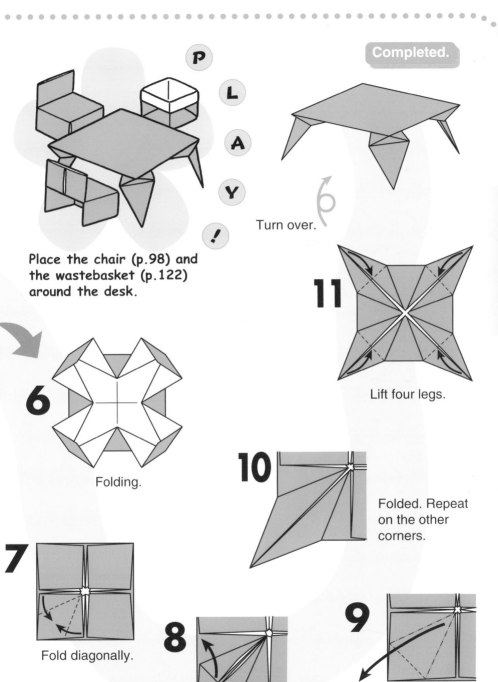

P
L
A
Y
!

Completed.

Turn over.

Place the chair (p.98) and
the wastebasket (p.122)
around the desk.

11 Lift four legs.

6 Folding.

10 Folded. Repeat
on the other
corners.

7 Fold diagonally.

8 Unfold.

9 Open and
squash.

Steps 8 - 10 show
part of the process.

Table

Paper **Any color**

2

Fold edges to center.

1

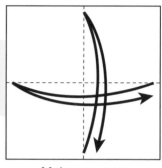

Make creases.

3

Fold to center.

5

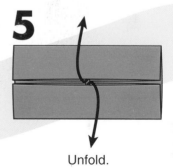

Unfold.

4

Fold to center.

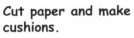

Cut paper and make cushions.

Completed.

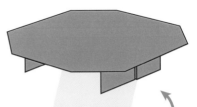

Completed.

Turn over.

8

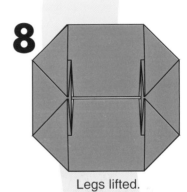

Legs lifted.

6

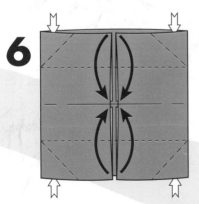

Open each corner and squash.

7

Fold and lift legs.

Bed

Paper | **Any color**

1

Fold in half to make a crease
and bring edges to center.

2

Fold at the
crease 3/8 fron
the edge.

3

Make creases

4

Fold each corner
into a triangle.

5

Fold over triangles.

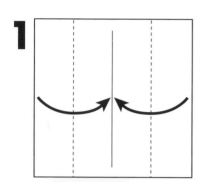
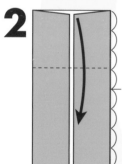
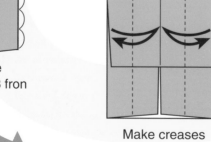
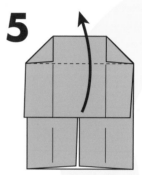

106

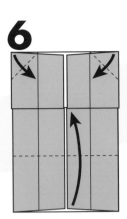

6

Fold top corners and
the bottom edge
upward.

7

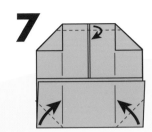

Fold the top edge a little
and bottom corners.

8

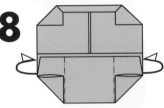

Fold the upper flaps
inward on creases.

9

Fold into the
pocket.

10

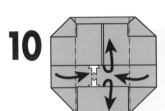

Fold the upper layer
upward and both sides
inward so that the whole
looks like a box.

Shift.

Completed.

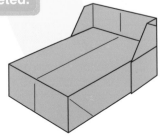

P L A Y !

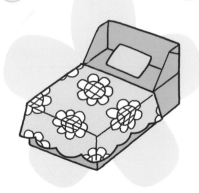

**Make a bed cover and a pillow
with other paper.**

OrganUIStringsan

Paper **Brown or black**

1

Fold in half and make a crease.

2

Fold to center.

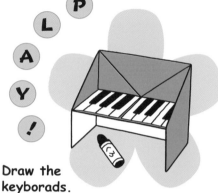

P L A Y !

Draw the keyboards.

3

Open and squash.

6

Folded.
Unfold and lift all.

Completed.

5

Fold both sides.

4

Fold upward.

House

Paper | **Any color**

1

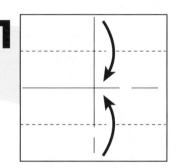

Make cross creases and fold in half.

2

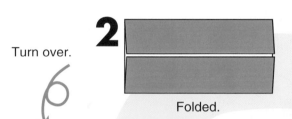

Folded.

Turn over.

3

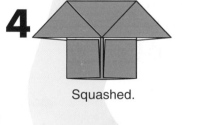

Open the side and squash the upper half.

4

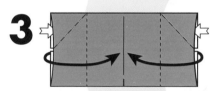

Squashed.

Completed.

Turn over.

P L A Y !

Draw the roof, window and front door.

Card case

Paper | **Any color**

1

Use paper 15 cm square. Fold on creases 1/5 from each edge.

2

Fold about 1/3 from the bottom edge.

3

Fold down 2/3 from the edge and insert into a pocket.

Completed.

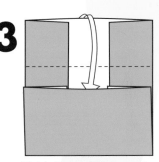

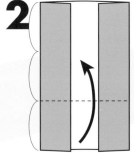

◀ ○ ○ **Card**

P
L
A
Y
!

If you use thick paper, it will be sturdy.

Greeting card

Paper | **Any color**

2

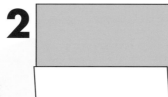

Folded.

3

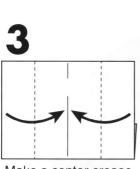

Make a center crease
and fold to center.

Turn over.

1

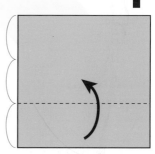

Fold on the creaese a little
less than 1/3 from the edge.

4

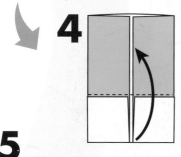

Fold
upward.

5

Fold and insert
into the pocket.

Completed.

P **L** **A** **Y** **!**

**Use lovely paper and write
your message on it.**

Tissue case

Paper | **Wrapping paper of B4 size**

1

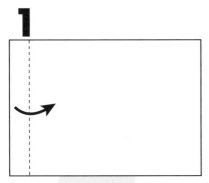

Fold on the crease 4 cm from the edge.

2

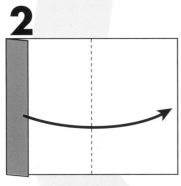

Fold in half.

4

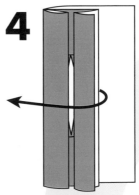

Fold over.

3

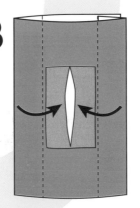

Tuck pocket tissue.

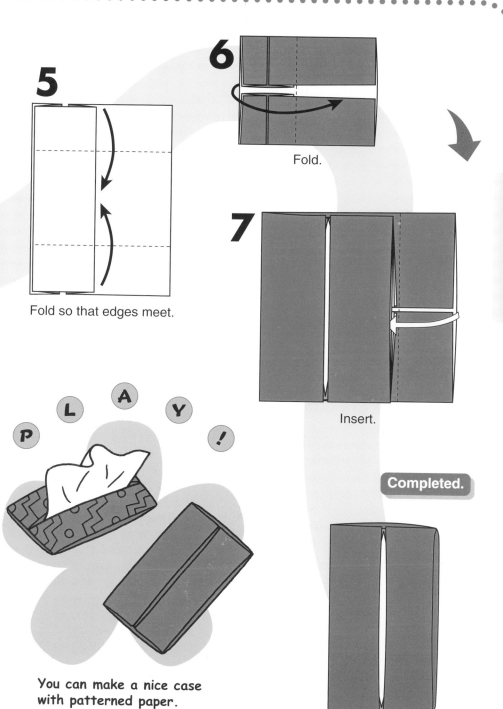

5

Fold so that edges meet.

6

Fold.

7

Insert.

Completed.

P L A Y !

You can make a nice case
with patterned paper.

Ring

Paper 7.5 x 4cm. Any color

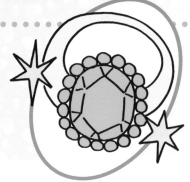

1

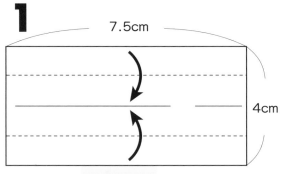

7.5cm

4cm

Fold in half to make a crease and bring edges to center.

2

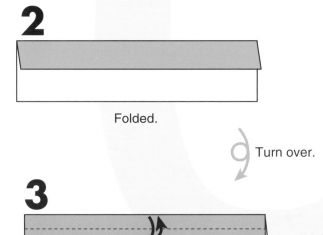

Folded.

Turn over.

3

Fold edges to center.

Turn over.

4

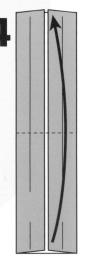

Fold in half.

5

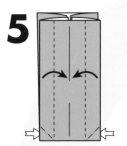

Fold upper flaps only. Open the bottom corners and squash.

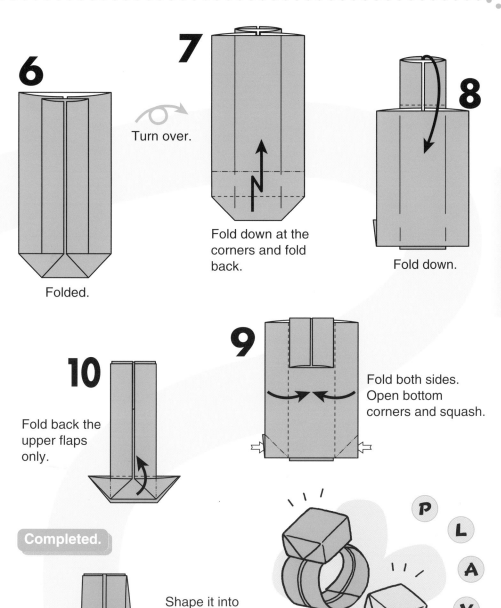

6

Folded.

7

Turn over.

Fold down at the corners and fold back.

8

Fold down.

9

Fold both sides. Open bottom corners and squash.

10

Fold back the upper flaps only.

Completed.

Shape it into a ring.

P L A Y !

Fold with white paper and paint the jewel part red or violet.

★ Give it to your father as a present. • • • • •

Necktie

Paper **Any color**

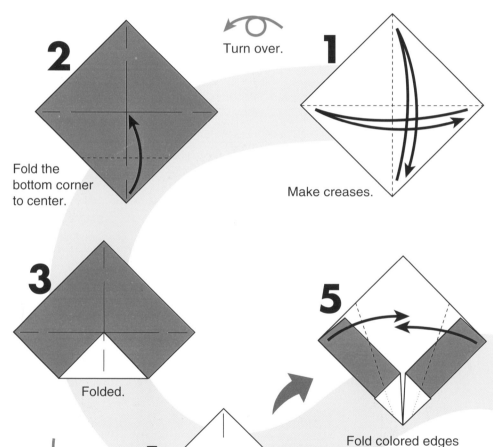

2

Fold the
bottom corner
to center.

Turn over.

1

Make creases.

3

Folded.

Turn over.

4

Fold the bottom
edge to center.

5

Fold colored edges
diagonally between
squares.

Completed.

Turn over.

11

Fold the top down.

10 Fold edges diagonally.

Turn over.

9

Folded.

P L A Y !

Try to fold it with stripe or polka-dot paper.

6 Fold again to make it slender.

7 Folded.

Turn over.

8 Fold upward.

Cup

Paper **Any color**

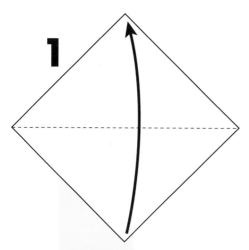

1

Fold into a triangle.

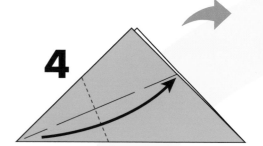

4

Fold the corner to the edge.

2

Fold so that edges meet.

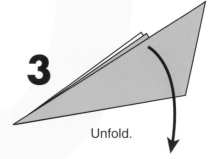

3

Unfold.

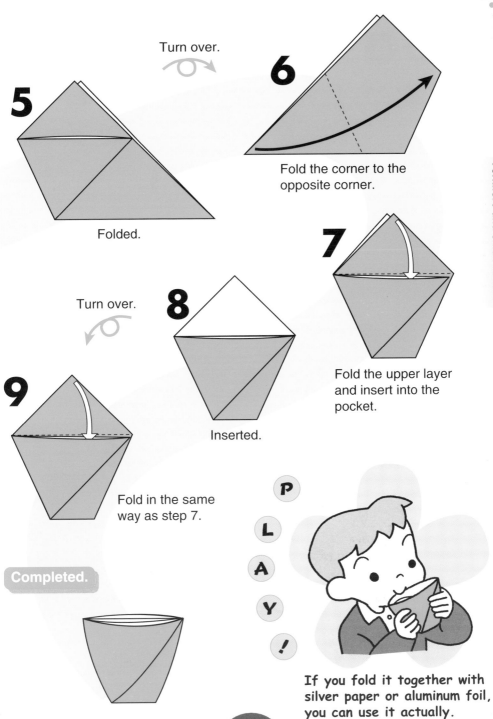

Turn over.

5

Folded.

6

Fold the corner to the opposite corner.

7

Fold the upper layer and insert into the pocket.

Turn over.

8

Inserted.

9

Fold in the same way as step 7.

Completed.

P L A Y !

If you fold it together with silver paper or aluminum foil, you can use it actually.

Furniture and Small Articles

Coaster

Paper | Any color

1

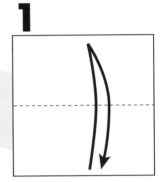

Fold in half.

2

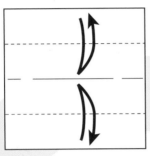

Make creases.

3

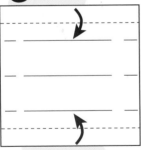

Fold edges to align with creases.

4

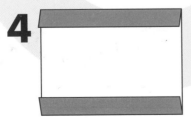

Folded.

Turn over.

Shift.

5

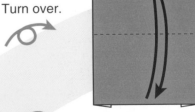

Fold in half to make a crease.

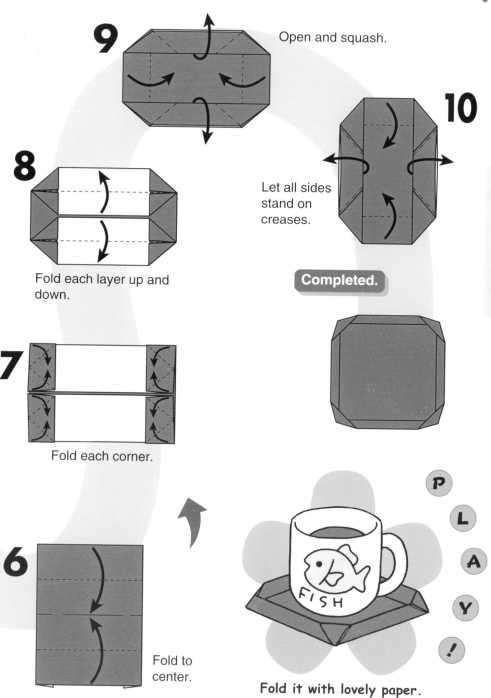

9

Open and squash.

10

Let all sides
stand on
creases.

8

Fold each layer up and
down.

Completed.

7

Fold each corner.

6

Fold to
center.

P
L
A
Y
!

FISH

Fold it with lovely paper.

Wastebasket

Paper | Newspaper

1

Fold in half.

2

Make a center crease and fold each corner into a triangle.

3

Fold the upper layer only.

4

Fold again.

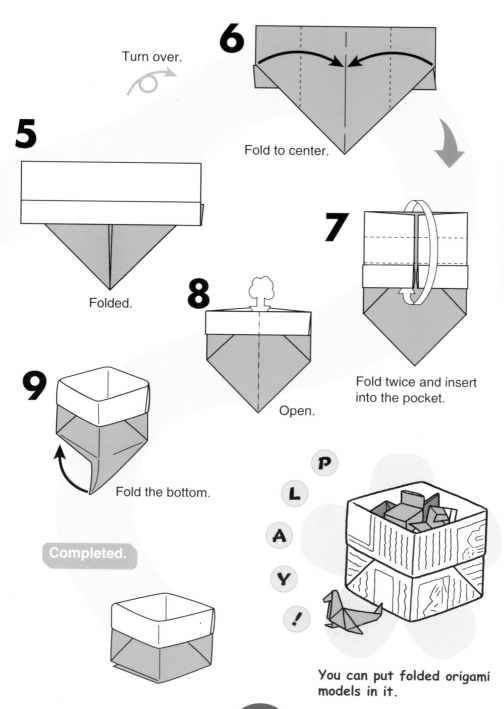

6

Fold to center.

5

Turn over.

Folded.

7

Fold twice and insert into the pocket.

8

Open.

9

Fold the bottom.

Completed.

P L A Y !

You can put folded origami models in it.

Small bowl

Paper | **Any color**

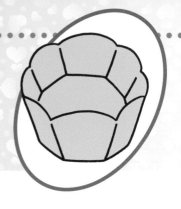

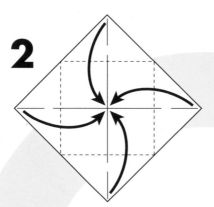

2

Fold each corner to center.

1

Make creases.

3

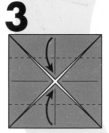

Fold to center.

6

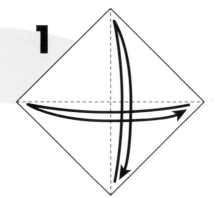

5

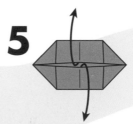

Unfold up and down.

Make creases.

4

Fold each corner.

Completed.

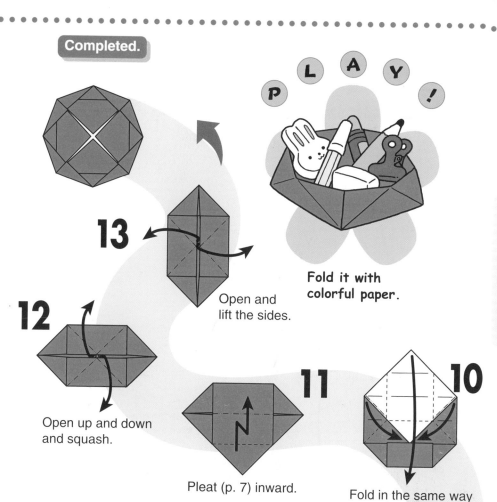

P L A Y !

Fold it with colorful paper.

13

Open and lift the sides.

12

Open up and down and squash.

11

Pleat (p. 7) inward.

10

Fold in the same way as steps 7 and 8.

7

Fold on the third crease from the bottom.

8

Fold the upper flaps inward on creases.

9

Fold the triangle and insert into the pocket.

Chopstick rest

Paper 7.5cm or 10cm square paper.

1

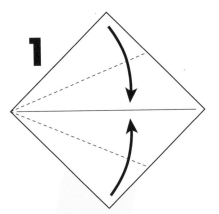

Make a center crease and fold edges to center.

2

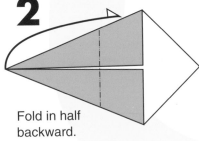

Fold in half backward.

3

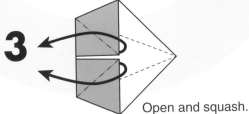

Open and squash.

6

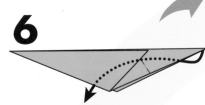

Inside reverse fold (p. 7)

5

Shift.

Fold in half.

4

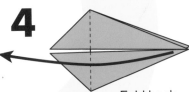

Fold back.

126

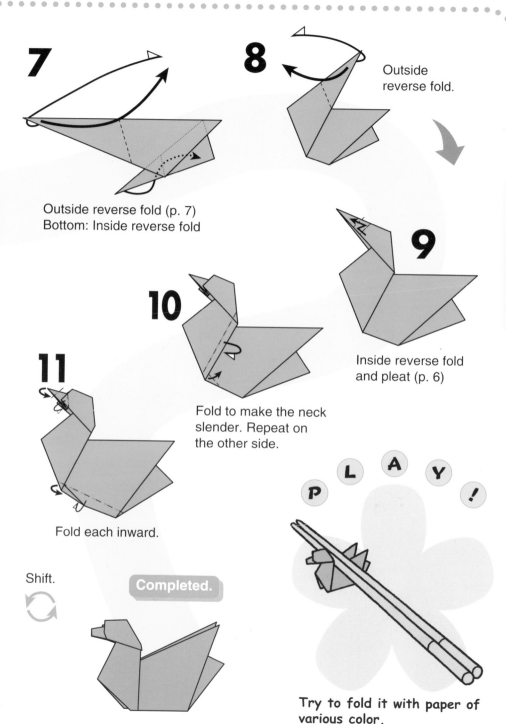

7

Outside reverse fold (p. 7)
Bottom: Inside reverse fold

8

Outside
reverse fold.

9

Inside reverse fold
and pleat (p. 6)

10

Fold to make the neck
slender. Repeat on
the other side.

11

Fold each inward.

Shift.

Completed.

P L A Y !

Try to fold it with paper of
various color.

Wallet

Paper **Any color**

1

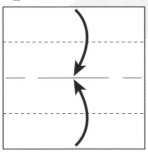

Fold in half to make a center crease. Bring edges to center.

2

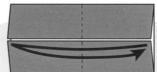

Fold in half to make a crease.

Turn over.

3

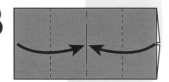

Fold to center.

4

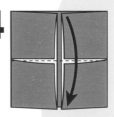

Fold in half.

Completed.

P L A Y !

Cut paper for money and insert in it.

Part 4

Cars, Ships, Airplanes

Lots of vehicles!

Automobile

Paper | **Any color**

1

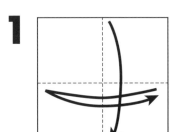

Make a vertical crease and fold in half.

2

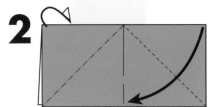

Fold one corner diagonally and the other corner backward.

3

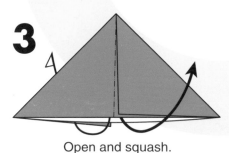

Open and squash.

5

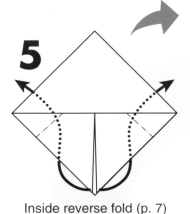

Inside reverse fold (p. 7)

4

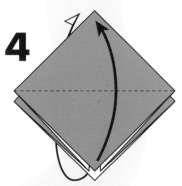

Fold upward. Repeat on the other side.

7

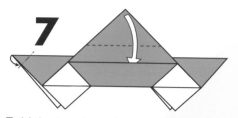

Fold the top down between the layers.
Make an inside reverse fold at the left corner.

8

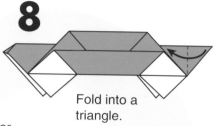

Fold into a triangle.

※Steps 9-12 show parts.

6

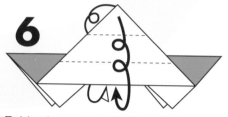

Fold twice so that the tires look square.
Repeat on the other side.

9

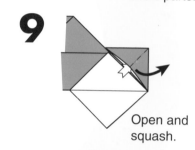

Open and squash.

10

Fold into a triangle.

11

Fold back.

12

Fold diagonally.
Repeat on the other side.

Completed.

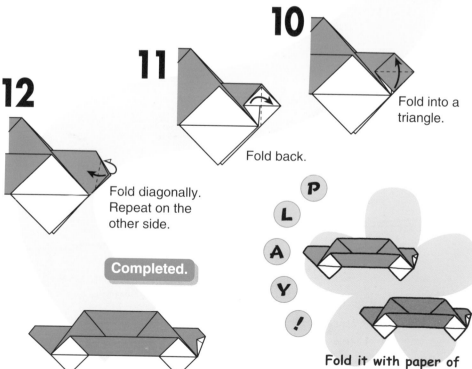

P L A Y !

Fold it with paper of various color.

131

Truck

Paper | **Any color**

1

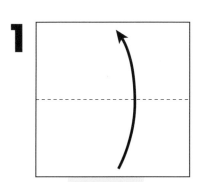

Fold in half.

2

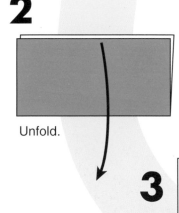

Unfold.

3

Fold on creases
1/3 from edges.

5

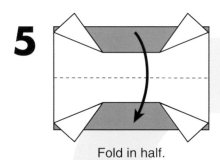

Fold in half.

4

Fold diagonally.

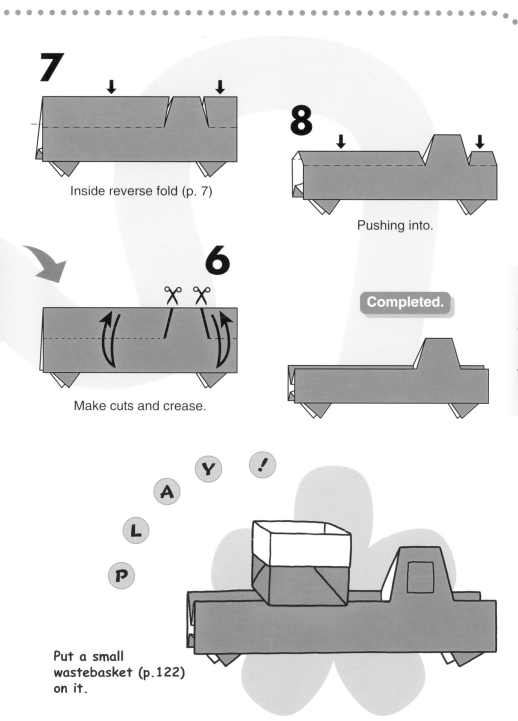

7

Inside reverse fold (p. 7)

8

Pushing into.

6

Make cuts and crease.

Completed.

A Y !
L
P

Put a small
wastebasket (p.122)
on it.

Patrol car

Paper | **Black**

1

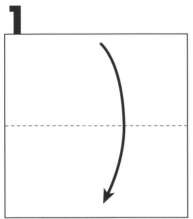

Fold in half.

2

Fold each corner of the upper layer into a triangle.

3

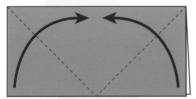

Fold so that the tip stick out a little.

4

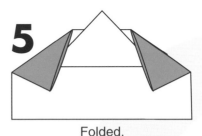

Fold each corner diagonally.

5

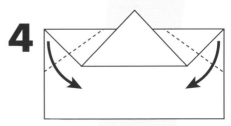

Folded.

134

Make a lamp with red paper and paste it on.

Turn over.

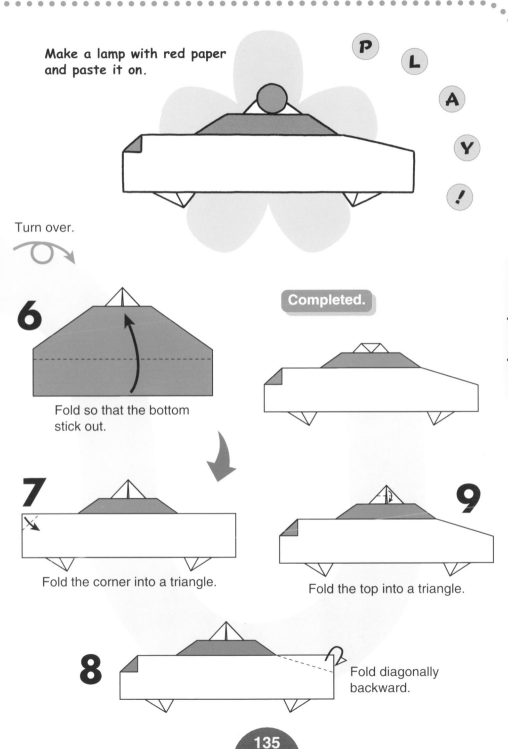

6

Fold so that the bottom stick out.

Completed.

7

Fold the corner into a triangle.

9

Fold the top into a triangle.

8

Fold diagonally backward.

Racing car

Paper | Any color

1

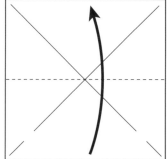

Make diagonal creases and fold in half.

2

Pleat (p. 6) in half.
Repeat on the other side.

3

Inside reverse fold (p. 7).
Repeat on the other side.

6

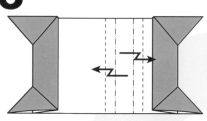

Pleat.

5

Fold so that back triangles appear.

4

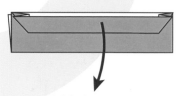

Folded. Unfold.

8

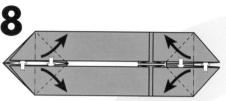

Open each corner and squash.

9

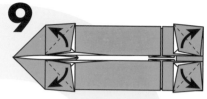

Fold each corner into a triangle.

7

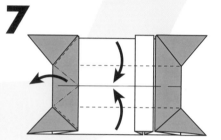

Pulling out the middle of left edge and fold in half.

10

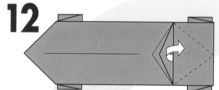

Folded.

Turn over.

11

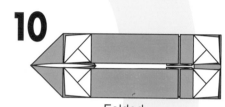

Dent the middle and lift both sides.

12

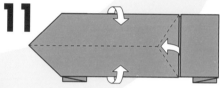

Dent the back and lift the backrest.

Completed.

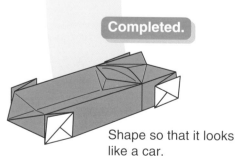

Shape so that it looks like a car.

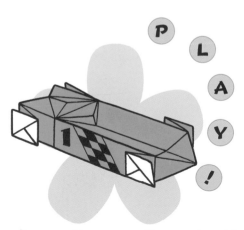

P L A Y !

Draw patterns you like on the side.

Motorcycle

Paper **Any color**

Body

1

First fold triangles and fold in half.

2

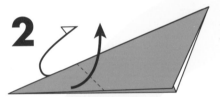

Make an outside reverse fold (p. 7) upright.

3

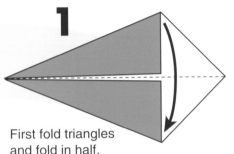

Make an inside reverse fold (p. 7) so that the top edge becomes level.

6

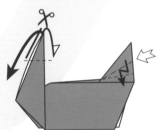

Body completed.

4

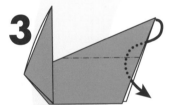

Inside reverse fold.

5

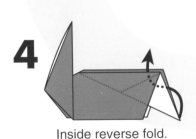

Make a cut in center and fold right and left.

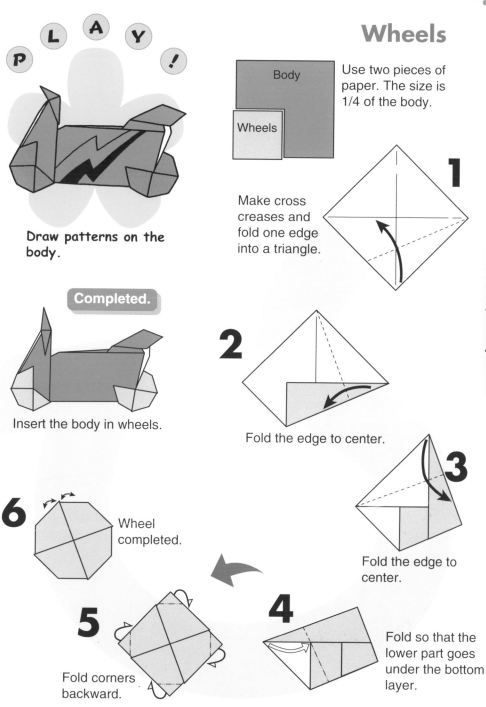

Wheels

P L A Y !

Draw patterns on the body.

Completed.

Insert the body in wheels.

Body

Wheels

Use two pieces of paper. The size is 1/4 of the body.

1

Make cross creases and fold one edge into a triangle.

2

Fold the edge to center.

3

Fold the edge to center.

4

Fold so that the lower part goes under the bottom layer.

5

Fold corners backward.

6

Wheel completed.

Passenger car

Paper **Any color**

1

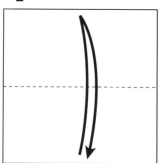

Make a crease.

2

Fold edges to center.

5

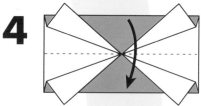

Make cuts along thick lines.

4

Fold in half.

3

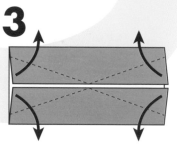

Fold diagonally.

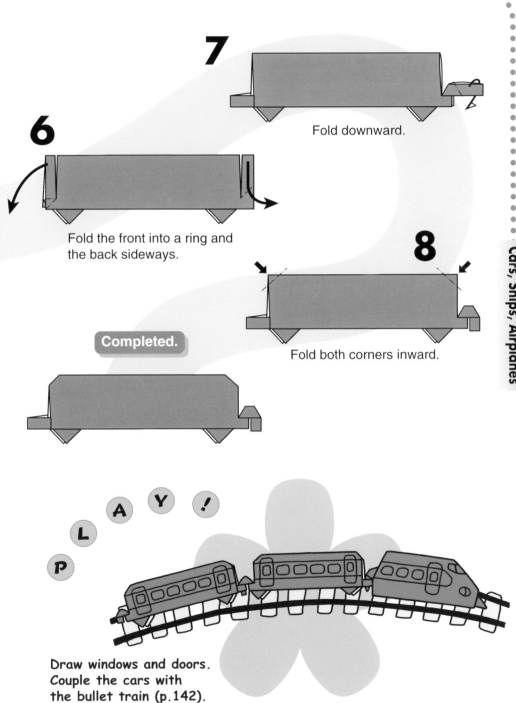

7

Fold downward.

6

Fold the front into a ring and the back sideways.

8

Fold both corners inward.

Completed.

P L A Y !

Draw windows and doors.
Couple the cars with
the bullet train (p.142).

Bullet train

Paper | White or blue

1

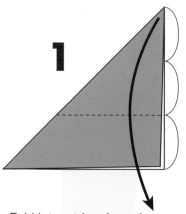

Fold into a triangle and then fold on a crease 1/3 from the edge.

2

Fold diagonally.

3

Fold so that edges align.

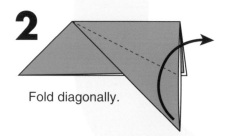

4

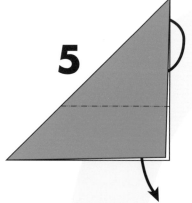

Unfold and return to step 1.

5

Make an inside reverse fold (p. 7) on creases.

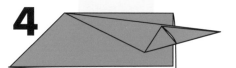

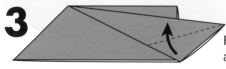

P L A Y !

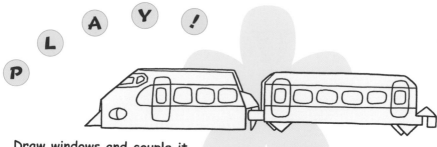

Draw windows and couple it with passenger cars (p.140).

6

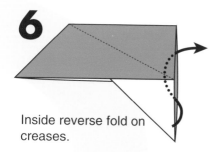

Inside reverse fold on creases.

Completed.

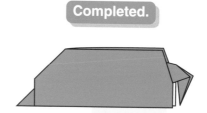

7

Fold inward.

11

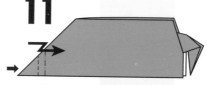

Push the corner in with pleat (p. 6).

8

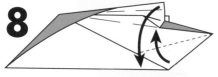

Folding. When folded, squash.

10

Fold inward.

9

Inside reverse fold.

Airplane

Paper **Any color**

1

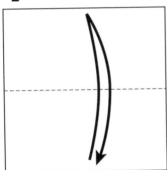

Make a crease.

2

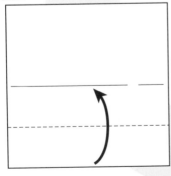

Fold the edge to center.

3

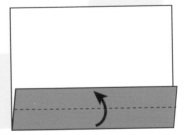

Fold again.

4

Fold again.

5

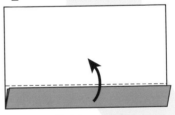

Folded.

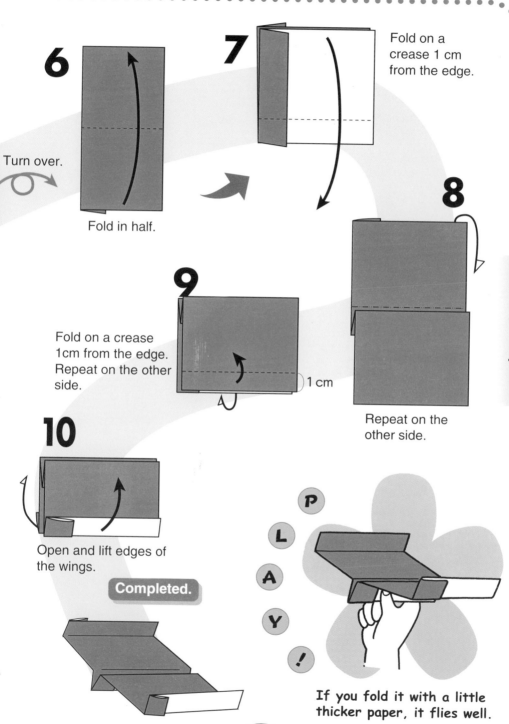

6

Turn over.

Fold in half.

7

Fold on a crease 1 cm from the edge.

8

Repeat on the other side.

9

Fold on a crease 1cm from the edge. Repeat on the other side.

1 cm

10

Open and lift edges of the wings.

Completed.

P L A Y !

If you fold it with a little thicker paper, it flies well.

Jet plane

Paper | **Any color**

1

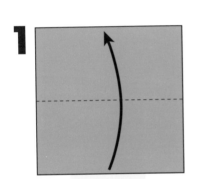

Fold in half.

2

Unfold.

3

Fold each corner into a triangle.

4

Fold the corner.

5

Turn over.

Folded.

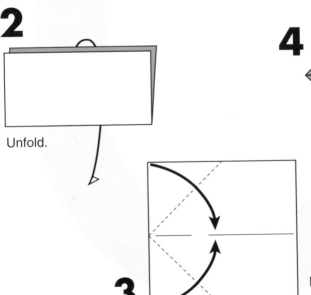

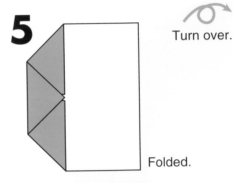

6

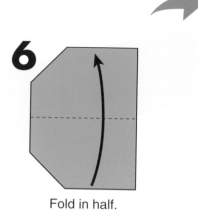

Fold in half.

7

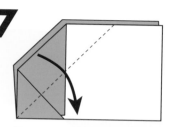

Fold so that edges align.

8

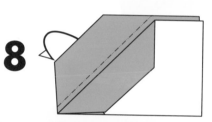

Repeat on the other side.

9

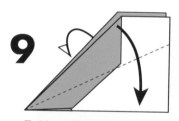

Fold so that edges align.
Repeat on the other side.

Completed.

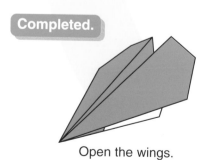

Open the wings.

P L A Y !

Draw national flags on the wing.

Hot-air balloon

Paper | Any color

2

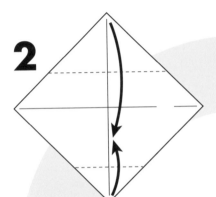

Fold corners into small and large triangles.

1

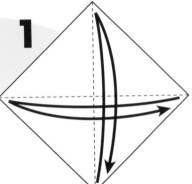

Make creases.

3

Fold corners backward.

5

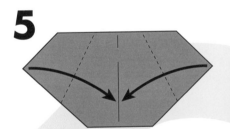

Fold edges to center.

4

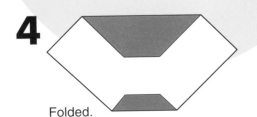

Folded.

Turn over.

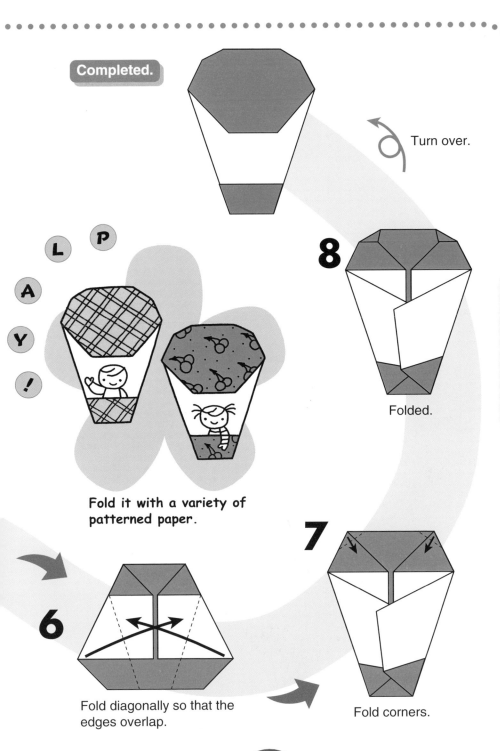

Completed.

Turn over.

8

Folded.

PLAY!

Fold it with a variety of patterned paper.

7

Fold corners.

6

Fold diagonally so that the edges overlap.

Rocket

Paper | **Silver or others**

1

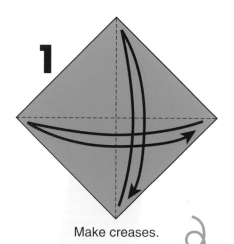

Make creases.

Turn over.

5

Repeat on all
other sides.

4

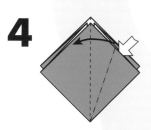

Open and squash.

2

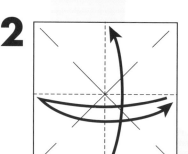

Make creases and fold in
half.

3

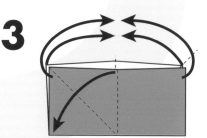

Pinch both corners, fold
on creases and squash.

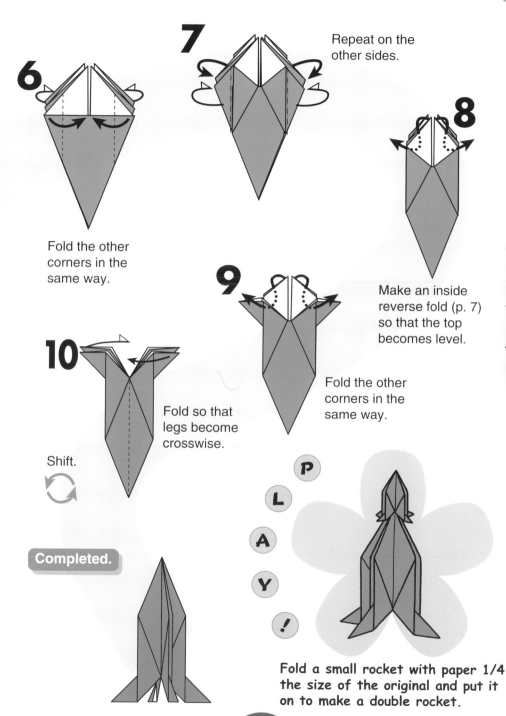

6

Fold the other corners in the same way.

7 Repeat on the other sides.

8 Make an inside reverse fold (p. 7) so that the top becomes level.

9 Fold the other corners in the same way.

10 Fold so that legs become crosswise.

Shift.

Completed.

P L A Y !

Fold a small rocket with paper 1/4 the size of the original and put it on to make a double rocket.

Motorboat

Paper | Any color

2

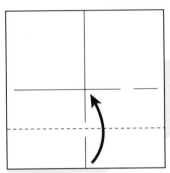

Fold the bottom edge to center.

1

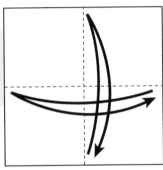

Make creases.

3

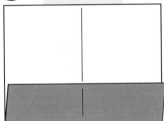

Folded.

Turn over.

5

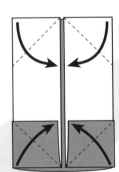

Fold each corner into a triangle.

4

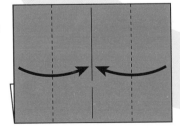

Fold to center.

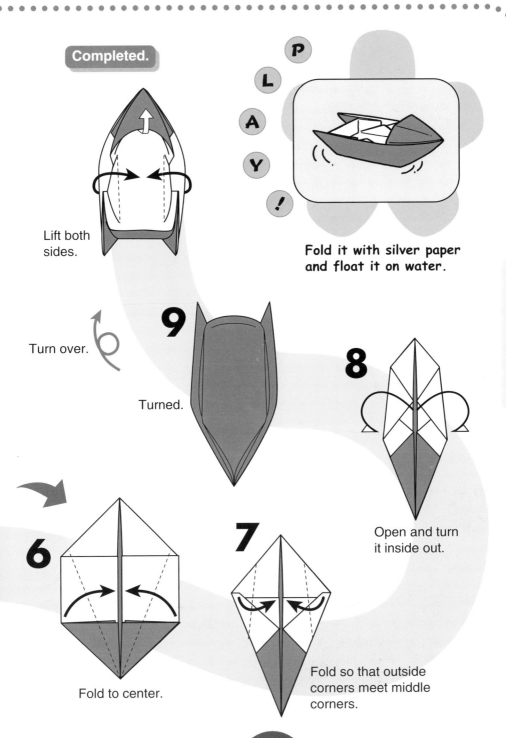

Completed.

Lift both sides.

P L A Y !

Fold it with silver paper and float it on water.

Turn over.

9 Turned.

8

Open and turn it inside out.

6 Fold to center.

7 Fold so that outside corners meet middle corners.

Sailboat

Paper | **Any color**

2

Fold to center.

1

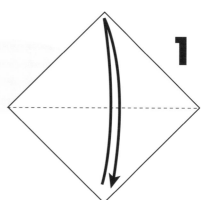

Make a crease.

3

Folded.

Turn over.

4

Fold in half.

5

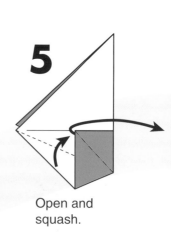

Open and squash.

154

Completed.

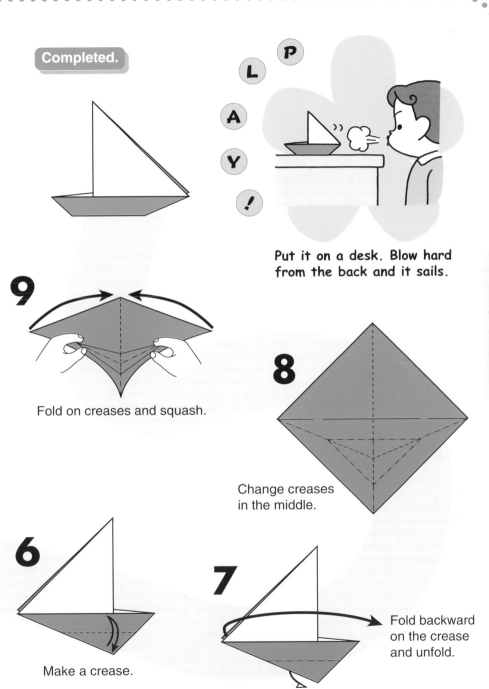

L P A Y !

Put it on a desk. Blow hard from the back and it sails.

9 Fold on creases and squash.

8 Change creases in the middle.

6 Make a crease.

7 Fold backward on the crease and unfold.

Catamaran

Paper **Any color**

1

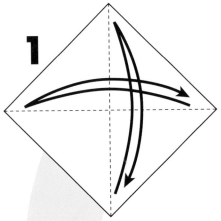

Make creases.

5

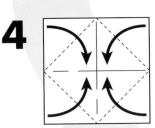

Unfold.
Return to step 1.

4

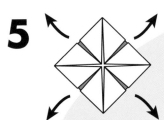

Fold corners to center.

Turn over.

2

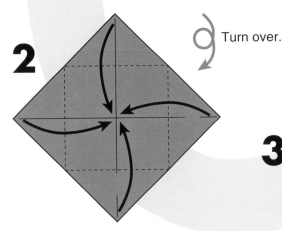

Turn over.

Fold four corners to center.

3

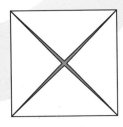

Folded.

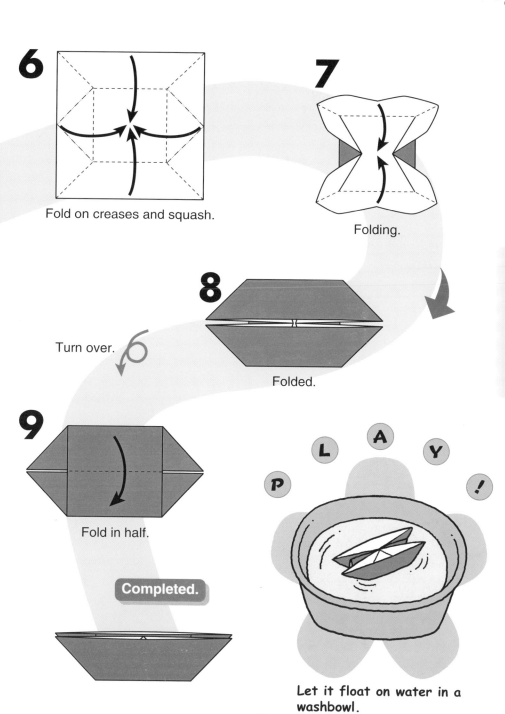

6

Fold on creases and squash.

7

Folding.

8

Turn over.

Folded.

9

Fold in half.

Completed.

P L A Y !

Let it float on water in a washbowl.

INDEX

About the author : Satoshi Takagi

Mr. Takagi was born in Kyoto in 1935. He graduated from the department of education of Kyoto University. He is a director of the Japan Origami Association. As an origami artist and researcher, he has devoted himself to the promotion of origami. He is playing an active part in various fields, including televisions, newspapers, magazines as well as lectures and exhibitions. He has authored a lot of origami books.

ORIGAMI BOOKS
from Japan Publications

3D ORIGAMI: Step-by-step Illustrations by Yoshie Hatahira et.al.
90 pp., 8 1/4 x 10 1/4 in., 24 pp. color, 64 pp. b/w photos and line drawings, paperback.
ISBN: 4-88996-057-0

BRILLIANT ORIGAMI: A Collection of Original Designs by David Brill
240 pp., 7 1/4 x 10 1/4 in., 8 pp. color, 215 pp. line drawings, paperback.
ISBN: 0-87040-896-8

CREATIVE ORIGAMI by Kunihiko Kasahara
180 pp., 8 1/4 x 11 3/4 in., 8 pp. b/w photos, 160 pp. line drawings, paperback.
ISBN: 0-87040-411-3

FABULOUS ORIGAMI BOXES by Tomoko Fuse
98 pp., 7 1/4 x 10 1/4 in., 8 pp. color, 80 pp. line drawings, paperback.
ISBN: 0-87040-978-6

HOME DECORATING WITH ORIGAMI by Tomoko Fuse
126 pp., 7 1/4 x 10 1/4 in., 16 pp. color, 104 pp. line drawings, paperback.
ISBN: 4-88996-059-7

KUSUDAMA: Ball Origami by Makoto Yamaguchi
72 pp., 7 1/4 x 10 1/4 in., 8 pp. color, 65 pp. line drawings, paperback.
ISBN: 4-88996-049-X

KUSUDAMA ORIGAMI by Tomoko Fuse
110 pp., 10 1/8 x 7 1/4 in., 8 pp. color, 81 pp. 2 color line drawings, paperback.
ISBN: 4-88996-087-2

MAGIC OF ORIGAMI, THE, by Alice Gray and Kunihiko Kasahara with cooperation of Lillian Oppenheimer and Origami Center of America
132 pp., 7 1/4 x 10 1/4 in., 122 pp. b/w photos and line drawings, paperback.
ISBN: 0-87040-624-8

ORIGAMI by Hideki Sakata
66 pp., 7 1/4 x 10 1/4 in., 66 pp. full color illustrations, paperback.
ISBN: 0-87040-580-2

ORIGAMI ANIMALS by Keiji Kitamura
88 pp., 8 1/4 x 10 1/4 in., 88 pp. full color illustrations, 12 sheets of origami paper included, paperback.
ISBN: 0-87040-941-7

ORIGAMI BOXES by Tomoko Fuse
72 pp., 7 1/4 x 10 1/4 in., 8 pp. color, 60 pp. line drawings, paperback.
ISBN: 0-87040-821-6

ORIGAMI CLASSROOM I by Dokuotei Nakano
Boxed set, board-book: 24 pp., 6 x 6 in., 24 pp. full color illustrations, plus origami paper: 6 x 6 in., 54 sheets of rainbow-color paper.
ISBN: 0-87040-912-3

ORIGAMI CLASSROOM II by Dokuotei Nakano
Boxed set, board-book: 24 pp., 6 x 6 in., 24 pp. full color illustrations, plus origami paper: 6 x 6 in., 60 sheets of rainbow-color paper.
ISBN: 0-87040-938-7

ORIGAMI FOR THE CONNOISSEUR by Kunihiko Kasahara and Toshie Takahama
168 pp., 7 1/4 x 10 1/4 in., 2 color line drawings, paperback.
ISBN: 4-8170-9002-2

ORIGAMI MADE EASY by Kunihiko Kasahara
128 pp., 6 x 8 1/4 in., 113 pp. b/w photos and line drawings, paperback.
ISBN: 0-87040-253-6

ORIGAMI OMNIBUS: Paper-folding for Everybody by Kunihiko Kasahara
384 pp., 7 1/4 x 10 1/4 in., 8 pp. color, 360 pp. line drawings, paperback.
ISBN: 4-8170-9001-4

ORIGAMI QUILTS
86 pp., 7 1/4 x 10 1/4 in., 8 pp. color, 73 pp. line drawings, paperback.
ISBN: 0-87040-868-2

ORIGAMI TREASURE CHEST by Keiji Kitamura
80 pp., 8 1/4 x 10 1/4 in., full color, paperback.
ISBN: 0-87040-868-2

PAPER MAGIC: Pop-up Paper Craft by Masahiro Chatani
92 pp., 7 1/4 x 10 1/4 in., 16 pp. color, 72 pp. b/w photos and line drawings, paperback.
ISBN: 0-87040-757-0

PLAYFUL ORIGAMI by Reiko Asou
96 pp., 8 1/4 x 10 1/4 in., 48 pp. full color illustrations, 10 sheets of origami paper included, paperback.
ISBN: 0-87040-827-5

POLYHEDRON ORIGAMI FOR BEGINNERS by Miyuki Kawamura
99 pp., 10 1/8 x 8 1/4 in., 51 pp. color, 48 pp. line drawings, paperback.
ISBN: 4-88996-085-6

POP-UP GIFT CARDS by Masahiro Chatani
80 pp., 7 1/4 x 10 1/4 in., 16 pp. color, 64 pp. b/w photos and line drawings, paperback.
ISBN: 0-87040-768-6

POP-UP GEOMETRIC ORIGAMI by Masahiro Chatani and Keiko Nakazawa
86 pp., 7 1/4 x 10 1/4 in., 16 pp. color, 64 pp. b/w photos and line drawings, paperback.
ISBN: 0-87040-943-3

POP-UP ORIGAMIC ARCHITECTURE by Masahiro Chatani
88 pp., 7 1/4 x 10 1/4 in., 4 pp. color, 11 pp. b/w photos, 68 pp. line drawings, paperback.
ISBN: 0-87040-656-6

QUICK & EASY MORE ORIGAMI
Boxed set, book: 62 pp., 6 x 6 in., 30 pp. color and 30 pp. line drawings, origami paper: 60 sheets in 6 colors.
ISBN: 4-88996-095-3

Quick & Easy ORIGAMI by Toshie Takahama
Boxed set, book: 60 pp., 6 x 6 in., 30 pp. color and 30 pp. line drawings, origami paper: 60 sheets in 6 colors.
ISBN: 4-88996-056-2

Quick & Easy ORIGAMI BOXES by Tomoko Fuse
Boxed set, book: 60 pp., 6 x 6 in., 30 pp. color and 30 pp. line drawings, origami paper: 60 sheets in 6 colors.
ISBN: 4-88996-052-X

UNIT ORIGAMI: Multidimensional Transformations by Tomoko Fuse
244 pp., 7 1/4 x 10 1/4 in., 8 pp. color, 220 pp. b/w photos and line drawings, paperback.
ISBN: 0-87040-852-6